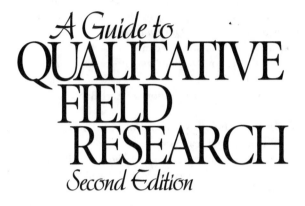

A Guide to
QUALITATIVE FIELD RESEARCH
Second Edition

Related Titles in Research Methods and Statistics from Pine Forge Press

Making Sense of the Social World, Second Edition by Daniel F. Chambliss and Russell K. Schutt

Investigating the Social World, Fifth Edition by Russell K. Schutt

The Practice of Research in Social Work by Rafael J. Engel and Russell K. Schutt

The Practice of Research in Criminology and Criminal Justice, Second Edition by Ronet K. Bachman and Russell K. Schutt

Designing Surveys: A Guide to Decisions and Procedures, Second Edition by Ronald F. Czaja and Johnny Blair

Adventures in Social Research, Fifth Edition by Earl Babbie, Fred Halley, and Jeanne Zaino

Adventures in Social Research with SPSS Student Version 11.0, Fifth Edition by Earl Babbie, Fred Halley, and Jeanne Zaino

Using SPSS for Social Statistics and Research Methods by Billy Wagner

Social Statistics for a Diverse Society, Fourth Edition by Chava Frankfort-Nachmias and Anna Leon-Guerrero

Social Statistics for a Diverse Society, Fourth Edition with SPSS Student Version 13.0 by Chava Frankfort-Nachmias and Anna Leon-Guerrero

Multiple Regression: A Primer by Paul Allison

Experimental Design and the Analysis of Variance by Robert K. Leik

How Sampling Works by Richard Maisel and Caroline Hodges Persell

Other Pine Forge Press Titles of Interest

Social Problems by Anna Leon-Guerrero

Sociology: Architecture of Everyday Life, Sixth Edition by David Newman

The McDonaldization of Society, Revised, New Century Edition by George Ritzer

This Book Is Not Required, Third Edition by Inge Bell, Bernard McGrane, and John Gunderson

Explorations in Classical Sociological Theory by Kenneth Allan

Sociology in the Classical Era by Laura Edles and Scott Appelrouth

Illuminating Social Life, Third Edition by Peter Kivisto

Race, Ethnicity, Gender, and Class, Fifth Edition by Joseph Healey

Diversity and Society by Joseph Healey

Production of Reality, Fourth Edition by Jodi O'Brien

Second Thoughts, Third Edition by Janet Ruane and Karen Cerulo

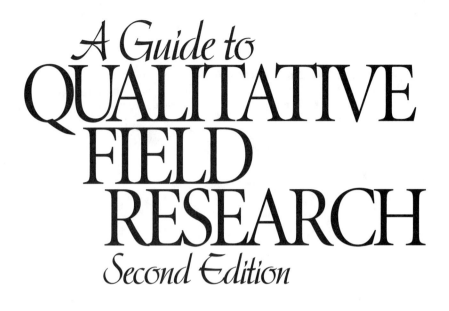

A Guide to
QUALITATIVE
FIELD
RESEARCH
Second Edition

Carol A. Bailey
Virginia Tech

PINE FORGE PRESS
An Imprint of Sage Publications, Inc.
Thousand Oaks • London • New Delhi

For information:

Pine Forge Press
A Sage Publications Company
2455 Teller Road
Thousand Oaks, California 91320
E-mail: order@sagepub.com

Sage Publications Ltd.
1 Oliver's Yard
55 City Road
London EC1Y 1SP
United Kingdom

Sage Publications India Pvt. Ltd.
B-42, Panchsheel Enclave
Post Box 4109
New Delhi 110 017 India

Printed in the United States of America.

Library of Congress Cataloging-in-Publication Data

Bailey, Carol A., 1950-
A guide to qualitative field research / Carol A. Bailey. — 2nd ed.
    p. cm.
Includes bibliographical references and index.
ISBN 1-4129-3650-0 or 978-1-4129-3650-7 (pbk.)
    1. Social sciences—Research—Methodology. I. Title.
H62.B275 2007
300.72′3—dc22   2006007756

This book is printed on acid-free paper.

            08   09   10   10   9   8   7   6   5   4   3   2

Acquisitions Editor:	Jerry Westby
Editorial Assistant:	Kim Suarez
Project Editor:	Tracy Alpern
Copy Editor:	Barbara Ray
Proofreader:	Amy Graham
Typesetter:	C&M Digitals (P) Ltd.
Indexer:	Kathy Paparchontis
Cover Designer:	Michelle Kenny

Contents

To Skip, Nicole, and Nicolai Fuhrman

About the Author

Carol A. Bailey is an Associate Professor of Sociology at Virginia Tech. She has won numerous teaching awards, including the university-wide Alumni Award for Teaching Excellence. She teaches undergraduate research methods and graduate-level courses on qualitative methodology and pedagogy for college teachers. Once the Director of the University Writing Program, she now primarily focuses on evaluating programs that serve children with severe mental illnesses and their families.

Preface

Although I wrote *A Guide to Qualitative Field Research* to provide students with clear, specific instructions about how to conduct field research, I find this purpose somewhat difficult to fulfill, because in many ways such a how-to guide is an oxymoron. Intangibles, such as luck, feelings, and timing, often are crucial features of research in natural settings. In truth, this volume cannot teach students who undertake field research how to deal with the unexpected, other than to warn them to be prepared for the inevitable. Nor can it teach many of the characteristics demanded of field researchers—good social skills, an ability to cope with ambiguity, patience, and flexibility. Basically, I believe that if you want to learn how to do field research, you have to *do* field research. Nonetheless, in spite of all the difficulties associated with writing a how-to guide to field research, I am going to blunder forward, because that is the sort of thing a field researcher does.

A second purpose of this guide is to help students develop analytic tools that they can use outside of the classroom. By becoming informed consumers of research, students gain the skills needed to evaluate the claims of politicians, advertisers, media pundits, parents, peers, and scientists of all types. Good research skills can help all of us be skeptical about conclusions that are based on limited and unsystematic observations. A little less certainty in our views about why people behave as they do is probably healthy.

This guide stresses how the same social forces that influence the rest of our lives affect field research. Ironically, the social nature of the research enterprise is often ignored in discussions of methodology. For example, although sociologists offer entire courses on stratification, those of us who teach social research methods sometimes act as though systems of inequality are irrelevant to methods. By understanding that field research is a social product, we become more capable of conducting and evaluating research.

Written from a sociological perspective, this book focuses on five major themes. First, because field researchers are simultaneously social scientists and human beings involved in long-term interpersonal relationships in natural settings, I emphasize ethical issues in every chapter. Once field research is rightfully situated in the larger social world, the salience and complexity of ethical issues in field research become acutely visible and can no longer be relegated to a single chapter.

Second, I do not separate the research process from the characteristics of those involved in it. Instead, I emphasize the myriad ways that status characteristics—age, gender, race, ethnicity, sexual orientation, and social class—affect the process of field research. For example, one's race may make gaining entrée in one setting difficult but facilitate entry in another setting; one's similarity in social class background with members in a setting may lead to levels of rapport and disclosure that could not be achieved by someone from another social class. Thus, I argue that what we learn as field researchers is, in part, a function of our personal and academic biographies.

Third, I view research as a nonlinear process. Field research is not performed in a series of stages or steps. In other words, the researcher does not complete one step or stage and then move on to the next one. Rather, the processes involved in field research are overlapping, ongoing, reciprocal, and embedded in each other. Although conventional book publishing techniques require that I present issues in a linear fashion, throughout this guide I stress the synergistic and reciprocal nature of the processes involved in research.

Fourth, I attempt to highlight the complexities, ambiguities, and diverse ways of conducting field research. Rather than masking the difficulties inherent in such research or concealing the academic controversies and debates internal to the field, I prefer to give beginning researchers a more realistic picture of its realities. Many of us believe that higher education should help students learn skills for adjudicating differences, resolving conflict, seeing other perspectives, weighing evidence, and valuing diversity. I do not believe we can help students learn these skills if we hide the messiness within our own academic gardens.

Finally, I hope to convey in this guide my passion for teaching so that it will inspire in students a passion for learning.

This second edition contains numerous additions and what I hope are improvements in the ground covered by the first version. In this edition, I

1. provide more coverage of diverse ways of conducting field research,

2. include a discussion of the American Sociological Association code of ethics,

3. extend the overview of paradigms,

4. upgrade examples and include more from dissertations,

5. expand the section on how to perform analysis,

6. enlarge the presentation on evaluation criteria.

In the process of editing and reevaluating this version of the guide, I am prompted to reconsider my own position as its creator. For that, I turn to the demands of field research itself. Good research often requires reflexivity: critically thinking and writing about who we are and how the choices we make affect our results. In addition, for me, it also calls for the sharing of one's values. Reflexivity and an awareness of one's values also are useful when one is writing a book about field research. As a slightly more than middle-aged, White, female sociologist, I take the value stance that sociology is at its best when it is contributing to improving the human condition. I suspect that by the end of the book the careful reader could determine that I focus primarily on ethnographies and evaluation research and that I value graduate education.

When I engage in reflexive thinking about this book, I realize that I have unintentionally selected and incorporated examples that reflect my interests but are not representative of the wide array of topics that field researchers study. Although I have worked to add examples from other specialty areas, I know that what I read for my classes and my research continues to dominate this text. Further, even though I have actively tried to pay more attention to the different ways of conducting field research, the book still reflects my areas of expertise. By engaging in this reflexive process, I have tried to produce a version more balanced than was the first edition. However, in the end I have come to accept the fact that in spite of these efforts, writing a book is much like conducting field research. Since there is no one right way to write it or one "truth" to be told, ultimately what is presented is a function of my training, worldview, and life experiences.

Acknowledgments

In addition to individuals acknowledged in the first edition, others assisted in the production of this version, and I want to extend my gratitude to them. I appreciate the thoughtful and helpful comments by numerous reviewers—Ronald Lukens-Bull, University of North Florida; George Martin, Montclair University; Larry Neuman, University of Wisconsin–Whitewater—and the infinite patience and assistance of Jerry Westby, Kim Suarez, Tracy Alpern, and Karen Wiley at Sage Publications/Pine Forge Press.

This guide benefits from being able to build upon the expertise of others, particularly Mitch Duneier*, Philippe Bourgois, Betty Russell, Elliot Liebow, and John Van Maanen. I quote liberally from these and other scholars as a way of allowing them to speak in their own words, which are invariably more powerful than my paraphrasing. I am grateful for having such a rich literature from which to draw.

None of my academic work—whether teaching, mentoring, research, service, or outreach—is independent of the positive influence of my mentor, J. Scott Long. I give thanks to Lisa Norris for her constant support and writing lessons. Trish Boyles gets mad props for providing song lyrics, diagrams, and insightful feedback on drafts, as does Adrienne Trier Bieniek for her careful reading of this guide. I am in awe of the editing skills possessed by Jennifer Mooney, who improved the substance and readability of this guide. Barbara Ray did a superb job of copyediting and taught me a lot in the process. Thanks to Andrea McIntire, Scott Cropper, Will McIntire, Sherrill Cropper, Rachael Stevens, Brenda Husser, Dianne Marshall, Trooper, Michelle Wooddell, Baggins, Richard Shaw, Cindy Broussard, and Nicolas Zeltvay. Nicole Fuhrman gets special recognition for typing the references.

My handsome husband, Ellsworth "Skip" Fuhrman, is my universe and continues to provide me with my day-to-day emotional sustenance. He enriches my life. His biggest gifts to me are Nicolai and Nicole. They, in turn, have taught me the meaning of joy.

---

* Various quotes from Duneier, M., *Sidewalk*, copyright © 1999, are reprinted with permission from Farrar, Straus and Giroux.

1

Introduction to Qualitative Field Research

Betty G. Russell lived with homeless women. She slept in shelters for the homeless, and she ate in soup kitchens. Russell, however, was not homeless; instead, she was a researcher who chose to explore and thus understand the lives of homeless women from their own perspectives. The methodology she used is known as *field research* (Russell, 1991).

Simply stated, field research is the systematic study of ordinary activities in the settings in which they occur. Its primary goal is to understand these activities and what they mean to those who engage in them. To gain this understanding, field researchers collect data by interacting with, listening to, and observing people during the course of their daily lives, usually in some self-contained setting, such as an elementary school classroom, a street corner, a car dealership, or a public housing community.

Just as survey research consists of more than asking a few people a few questions, field research involves much more than hanging out with, talking to, and watching people. Both methods of research are complicated and systematic, with clearly defined procedures to follow. Yet, at the same time, field research requires flexibility, because it can be chaotic, emotional, dangerous, and lacking in rigid rules to guide some aspects of the research process. In fact, luck, ambiguity, time constraints, and feelings often affect the planning, execution, and analysis of field research, making it all the more important for the researcher to be well prepared and trained in this methodology before engaging in it.

I highly recommend that before starting your own field research project, you take the time to read the guide in its entirety. Because field research is not conducted in stages, you will benefit from fully understanding the entire process prior to designing your own field research project.

In this chapter, I provide an overview of field research, and then I introduce to you the first of several themes integrated throughout this guide: the effects of status characteristics on the field research process. I hope that after reading this chapter, you will be better able to visualize the "big picture" and thus be more capable of understanding the specific details and instructions offered in subsequent chapters.

Overview

Field research* is the systematic study, primarily through long-term, face-to-face interactions and observations, of everyday life. A primary goal of field research is to understand daily life from the perspectives of people in a setting or social group of interest to the researcher. Field research is classified as a longitudinal research design because data collection can take a long time—usually months or years.

Naturalistic Setting

One of the distinguishing features of field research is where it is conducted. During field research, data are collected in the setting of the phenomenon of interest. For example, in her study of homeless women, instead of asking the women to come to her office, Russell (1991) went directly to them, to the shelters that served as their temporary homes. Field researchers go to myriad locations, from city council meetings to racetracks, from television stations to beauty pageants. They observe factory workers, dogcatchers, tattoo artists, drug dealers, and flight attendants.

Research conducted "in the field" is referred to as **naturalistic** inquiry because it does not require people in the setting of interest to deviate from their daily routines during the research. Data collected in this way provide a more holistic picture of people and their lives than what could be obtained from asking them to participate in an experiment or complete a survey about everyday events. Instead of looking at a limited number of preselected variables, as survey researchers must do, field researchers derive understanding from the larger, complicated, multifaceted, social,

---

* Boldface terms in the text are defined in the Glossary.

and historical contexts within which people's lives unfold. Field researchers pay attention to the temporal order of events and to changes over time. They believe that life is, metaphorically, better captured by a movie than by a photograph.

Rather than controlling events, the field researcher attempts to become part of the setting, with the goal of providing in-depth descriptions and analytical understandings of the meanings participants in a setting attach to their interactions and routines. The field researcher does this by becoming directly involved with the people in the setting and personally experiencing parts of their daily lives (Neuman, 1991). For example, Russell (1991) was concerned with how homeless women live from day to day; thus, for her data collection she volunteered for four months at a day shelter, where she could directly observe the women in their roles as residents of the shelters, diners at soup kitchens, participants in social activities, and mothers of children. Russell held babies, poured coffee, and chatted with shelter women. To discover how they found food, where they bathed or did their laundry, and how they coped with the routine and problematic events of their daily lives, she not only observed but also talked to them (Russell, 1991). She wished to know what these women did each day, but she also wanted to explore how they made sense of their lives and how they viewed themselves and other homeless women. It was through her participation at the shelter that Russell gained answers to her questions.

During his field research, Mitch Duneier became involved in the daily activities of street vendors—individuals selling books and magazines—on Sixth Avenue in Greenwich Village. He began his research as a customer then moved to an assistant (scavenging magazines from the trash, going for coffee, watching the tables), until he eventually worked as a full-time magazine vendor (Duneier, 1999, p. 11). Duneier's continual presence on the streets over several years allowed him to become privy to events, conversations, and rhythms of life among the vendors and panhandlers.

Over a five-year period, Philippe Bourgois spent hundreds of nights on the streets and in crack houses in East Harlem while conducting his field research. As a result of his immersion in their world, Bourgois was able to gain access to intimate moments in the lives of some of the participants. He

> visited [participants'] families, attending parties and intimate reunions—from Thanksgiving dinners to New Year's Eve celebrations. [He] interviewed, and in many cases befriended, the spouses, lovers, siblings, mothers, grandmothers, and—when possible—the fathers and stepfathers of the crack dealers. (1995, p. 13)

He observed, interviewed, and took photographs of them, even one of "Primo feeding cocaine to Caesar on the benches of a housing project courtyard" (p. 101).

Purpose of Research and Research Questions

Although all field research takes place within natural settings, it serves different purposes. It is well suited for, but not restricted to, descriptive or exploratory research. Generating theory is another frequent motivation for engaging in field research. Evaluation researchers and activist researchers are among those who often choose this method to generate data for their projects. Field research is sometimes used in the search for cause-and-effect relationships.

The primary reason for engaging in field research is to answer questions. Without research questions, the researcher—particularly one at the beginning of his or her career—most likely would be adrift in the setting for a long time before stumbling across a focus. Although experienced researchers might enter a setting without research questions and undertake their endeavors successfully, I do not recommend this course of action for undergraduate students—and I have never seen a committee approve a thesis or dissertation proposal without well-articulated research questions.

Field researchers usually begin their study with an overarching question, issue, or problem that leads to more specific research questions. For example, Duneier began his work with a focus on the moral order of the street vendors (1999, p. 9). As his research progressed, it was guided by the question of what relationships or tensions existed between the vendors and those who attempted to regulate the sidewalk space. He later asked even more specific questions, such as why are the informal mechanisms of social control not able to regulate the interactions between the men and women pedestrians (p. 190)?

Some researchers change their original research questions during the course of their work, and it is common to add, refine, or delete questions while in the field. Even though the flexible and emergent nature of fieldwork allows for the modification of research questions while research is on-going, if you are undertaking field research, I recommend that you seek approval from your instructor or graduate committee before you change your research questions.

Data

To answer their research questions, field researchers collect data primarily through systematic observations and interactions. In fact, observations using sight, sound, touch, taste, and smell are crucial to this type of research. Field researchers sometimes observe at predetermined times; they actively seek out interactions with particular people. Alternatively, the interactions and observations of the field researcher might be more flexible. Frequently, researchers simply try to be around the setting as often as possible. They might not have a standardized checklist of behaviors to observe; rather, the events in the setting determine both the nature of the interactions and what is observed.

In addition to interactions and observations, field researchers sometimes use other methods to gain insight into a setting. **Unstructured, semistructured,** and **structured interviews** are common techniques for supplementing observations. For example, Russell (1991) held semistructured interviews with 22 women, 10 more than once, and unstructured interviews with 50–60 women.

Interaction, observation, and interviewing are not the only techniques adopted by the field researcher. Researchers might analyze the content of documents or give out surveys to some individuals in a setting. Russell (1991), for instance, includes in her book the results of a survey she gave to 100 women. As this example illustrates, the data field researchers use can be amenable to statistical analysis, further blurring the distinction between qualitative and quantitative methods.

Data collected by the field researcher might also consist of the text of conversations among members in a setting. This type of research is called **conversational analysis.** Although Duneier's (1999) study of the men and women who sold books on the sidewalks of Greenwich Village was not primarily a conversational analysis, he included conversational analysis in an effort to provide additional insight into why some women felt threatened by encounters with one of the men on the sidewalk. Researchers who conduct conversational analysis might tape-record conversations for rigorous analysis, measuring even the briefest of pauses between speakers.

The types of data collected depend on the purposes of the specific field research project and the research questions that drive it. The bulk of data used for analysis by field researchers consists of nonnumeric texts— words, sentences, and observational and interview notes. The data collected by the researcher often result in many pages of observation and **field notes,** as well as transcripts of interviews and conversations.

Analysis

Trying to make sense of the massive amount of data and reducing it to meaningful accounts usually is a difficult, but often interesting, task.

Usually, data from fieldwork are analyzed inductively. Researchers engage in the rigorous process of **coding** as a mechanism for identifying portions of the data potentially useful for analysis. A researcher might then create a typology or develop themes from the data. Some researchers refine their hypotheses on the basis of the data, whereas others highlight key events, divergent findings, daily routines, and important processes. Field researchers often write their final manuscript in the form of engaging narratives that include detailed descriptions and key conceptual and theoretical implications of their work.

Ultimately, the researcher determines what is learned from field research. The researcher asks the questions, conducts the observations, and engages in the interactions. The project's data include the researcher's field notes. The researcher also analyzes the data, interprets them, and creates the final manuscript. Because of the central role played by the researcher in generating and analyzing the data, he or she is referred to as the research instrument. Thus, to a much greater degree than in other forms of research, field research is influenced by the characteristics of the researcher.

For the production of knowledge through field research, the researcher's history, personality, values, training, and status characteristics—gender, race, ethnicity, age, sexual orientation, and social class—become particularly relevant (Warren, 1988). What **participants** in the setting are willing to say and allow the researcher to observe will not be the same for all researchers. In other words, different researchers in the same setting will elicit different information from the participants. Additionally, what the researcher considers important enough to include in the field notes might vary. For example, in field notes, one researcher might highlight a detail that another might overlook or consider irrelevant.

In addition to researchers' personal characteristics informing data collection, they enter into the interpretive process and thus affect what is learned. Because the researcher is so central to this type of research, from the inception of the project to the final manuscript, many field researchers engage in the practice of **reflexivity**.

Reflexivity

Reflexivity is, in part, critically thinking about how one's status characteristics, values, and history, as well as the numerous choices one has made during the research, affect the results. As a result of the reflections, sometimes the researcher takes action, such as asking for assistance with some parts of the research or changing some facet of the research design. Then, in order to provide readers with information that can help them judge the quality of the final manuscript, researchers include relevant parts of the reflections. Whether researchers include their reflections in their final manuscript is often dependent on the paradigm that guides the research.

Paradigms

The procedures for conducting field research are complicated because they depend on the **paradigm** employed by the researcher. For example, some field research is conducted within a **positivist** paradigm, which has a commitment to objectivism, value-free research, and reliability. Alternatively, many field researchers adhere to an **interpretive** paradigm, which holds that social reality is not independent of the social meaning given to it by those in the setting. One of the many differences among the paradigms is the role of values in the research.

Values

The role of values in field research presents an ongoing area of disagreement among practitioners. I am drawn to field research because moral neutrality is not always a methodological requirement. I am among the group of researchers who believe that field research can help illuminate the life experiences of groups who are absent from much research. My hope is to provide insights into what might otherwise have been invisible, while knowing that the experience of others can be at best only represented, not captured, by field researchers. During some research projects, though, my values play a less important role. However, since I know that I am not value neutral in some of the work I conduct, I include a discussion of my value stance in some of my manuscripts.

In contrast, for some researchers, the quest for value neutrality is a hallmark of good qualitative research. Such researchers are less apt to include reflexive statements about values in their final manuscripts.

Final Manuscript

Field researchers usually publish their results in the form of journal articles, master's theses, dissertations, books, or technical reports—the same outlets available to other methodologies. However, the analysis strategies used and the presentation of the results can look considerably different. For example, dissertations using secondary data often have the chapter headings *Introduction* or *Statement of the Problem, Theory, Literature Review, Methods, Results, Discussion,* and *Conclusions.* Although field researchers can use these standard titles, they are less likely to do so. For instance, for her dissertation, Tiffany Chenault (2004) conducted a two-year study of the disjunctions between what was expected of a resident council in a public housing community and what it actually did. Her dissertation chapter headings included *Just Getting Started, The Voices of Rivertown,* and *Centering the Council.*

Overview Summary

Prior to engaging in it, one can rarely predict the fieldwork experience. Field research can be exciting or tedious, cheap or expensive, easy or difficult. It can result in the creation of a friendship—or the loss of one. The research results might confirm the researcher's expectations or be full of surprises.

Graduate students often say that they feel overwhelmed and lost while conducting field research. They report having almost a constant fear that they did not know what they were doing and felt fairly certain they were not doing it "right." These same students also tell me, though, that at some point their efforts began to make sense. That is the point where most of us who engage in field research start to have fun.

Field research is not restricted to academics or to any one discipline within academia; for example, students in nursing, education, anthropology, management, hospitality and tourism, Africana studies, communications, and sociology all conduct field research. However, different academic disciplines have developed different field research traditions, and there is not always consistency even within a discipline (Denzin & Lincoln, 1994). Furthermore, the standards for field research have changed historically, and the exemplars in the early field research literature are methodologically different from those of today. One of the reasons for the diversity within field research lies in its history.

History of Field Research

Writing about the history of field research is challenging because no definitive study has been undertaken into the origins of this strategy of inquiry

(Flick, von Kardorff, & Steinke, 2004), and authors disagree about when it was first done. Some scholars say that field research first appeared at the end of the 18th century; this group takes the position that field research is primarily an academic activity. Others, however, argue that this form of knowledge production existed long before it became the territory of academics.

Those discussing the history of fieldwork often refer to the work of Rosalie Wax. In a chapter in *Doing Fieldwork: Warnings and Advice,* Wax (1971) argues that some of the earliest descriptions of social settings date back to the fifth century B.C. She provides as an example of early fieldwork the report made by Herodotus to his readers that the Scythians collected the scalps of their enemies and made drinking cups from their skulls. Wax also writes that Romans in 37 A.D., Chinese in the fifth century, and Islamic traders and ambassadors in the eighth century wrote descriptions of other cultures, and European explorers, missionaries, government officials, and traders engaged in field research for the first time in the 13th century. Wax asserts that British and French field researchers also were conducting field research within their own countries as early as the latter part of the 18th century. For example, with the goal of "improving the conditions of the poor and working classes," researchers during this time period studied the conditions of hospitals, agricultural practices, illnesses of prisoners, and the lifestyles of prostitutes (Wax, 1971, p. 24).

In contrast to Wax's views, Flick, von Kardorff, and Steinke (2004) suggest that field research and other qualitative methods did not exist until the birth of the social sciences in the 19th century. One of the first sociologists to engage in field research was Harriet Martineau (1802–1876), who during the two years she spent traveling in the United States in the early 1800s (1834–1836) paid particular attention to the lives of women and children. En route to America, she began what would in its final form be considered one of the first sociological guides to field research, *How to Observe Morals and Manners* (1838). In this book she codifies the procedures that the foreign traveler should follow in observing and discovering ways of life different from one's own. Martineau's work arrived at a time when British travelers in particular were beginning to make odysseys abroad that combined pleasure with observation. After their journeys, many of these travelers—a great number of whom were women—recorded their observations in travel narratives that captured sociological features of the peoples among whom they lived (J. Mooney, personal communication, July 15, 2005).

Later in the 19th century, two of Martineau's fellow Britons, Charles Booth (1840–1916) and Beatrix Potter (1866–1943), contributed studies based on field research among the London working class. Booth, a wealthy Londoner, conducted a systematic study of London laborers. The resulting publication was the 17-volume *Life and Labour of the People of London* (1891–1903). His field research, which included living with workingmen's families, eventually led to the Old Age Pensions Act (1908) that established minimum wages, unemployment insurance, and state coverage for the sick and disabled (J. Mooney, personal communication, July 15, 2005).

Although Potter, the daughter of an industrial magnate, is best known for her work as a children's author (she produced the "Peter Rabbit" series of stories), she engaged in field research when she took a job as a sewing machine operator in a London sweatshop in order to observe firsthand the trials of factory life. She hoped that by experiencing the working conditions herself, she would be in a better position to document them and to work toward meaningful change (J. Mooney, personal communication, July 15, 2005; Wax, 1971).

One of the first anthropologists to live with people from other cultures was British social anthropologist Bronislaw Malinowski (1884–1942), who during the first half of the 20th century collaborated with his students and colleagues to produce many influential field studies (Wax, 1971). One of Malinowski's main contributions was convincing researchers that instead of being "armchair anthropologists" who studied other cultures by reading the narratives of competent informants, they should undertake intensive studies of other contemporary cultures: live with the people, learn their language, and experience every facet of their daily lives. Another anthropologist from this period was the German Franz Boas (1858–1942), who mentored other well-known anthropologists such as Ruth Benedict (1887–1948), Zora Neale Hurston (1891–1960), and Margaret Mead (1901–1978).

Around the same time in the United States, several sociologists, including Robert Ezra Park (1864–1944) at the University of Chicago, systematically observed ethnic enclaves, religious communities, occupational associations, and mental institutions in Chicago. In spite of the simultaneous growth of survey research and statistical techniques of data analysis, interest in field research quickly spread beyond Chicago and continues, with varying levels of acceptance, to this day (Neuman, 1991).

Disagreeing about when field research actually began is only one of many areas of contention among field researchers. As you read this guide, you will realize that the "field" of field research is somewhat messy (Denzin & Lincoln, 1994). For example, scholars continue to debate about what field research is, how it should be conducted, how it should be evaluated, and how ethical issues should be resolved. Rather than cleaning up this mess for you, I prefer to highlight points of disagreement and introduce alternative perspectives. Also, I think it is important to devote some time to one component of field research about which most scholars agree: It is affected by the status characteristics of the researcher.

Status Characteristics

Sociologists frequently look at the effects of **status characteristics**—gender, race, ethnicity, social class, sexual orientation, and age—on life experiences. A large body of empirical evidence indicates that status characteristics structure nearly every aspect of everyday life. For example, gender is related to such things as occupational patterns, wage distributions, likelihood of being interrupted when talking, and risks of personal violence. Women tend to be clustered in fewer occupations than men, they are more apt to be interrupted in mixed groups than are men, and they have a greater risk than men of being raped but a lower risk of being murdered. Race and ethnicity are related to residential segregation, quality of educational experiences, job opportunities, and access to health care.

The effects of status characteristics on life chances are far more complex than is implied by the above paragraph, primarily because individuals possess multiple characteristics simultaneously. We do not have either a gender or a race; instead, we have both. We concomitantly have an age, a sexual orientation, and a social class and live in a particular place in a specific historical period. Many of us have an ethnicity that is important to us. The combination of these characteristics affects our life chances.

Status characteristics affect almost every part of the field research process. For example, when one is conducting field research, one frequently engages in gendered interactions, gendered conversations, and gendered interpretations (Warren, 1988, p. 10). One's gender can influence which aspects of a setting one will come to know and how one will interpret experiences in that setting. Thus, gender can affect the production of knowledge. Simultaneously, the intersection of gender and other status characteristics can influence the research process.

Clearly, an analysis of the gender/field research nexus is much broader than I can discuss here. A complete review of gender and field research would need to address, at a minimum, how changing definitions of gender have corresponded with who does field research, how it is done, what is considered worthy of study, what is learned and for what purpose, how the final product is written, and how the work ultimately is evaluated. An examination of other characteristics would be equally complex.

Summary

This chapter has provided you with an overview of field research and an introduction to the theme of status characteristics and field research. You may have correctly surmised from this chapter that a "how-to guide" to field research is somewhat of a contradiction given the complexity of the subject and the lack of unified standards governing it. In fact, rigid rules are ineffective for many aspects of the research process. Field research simply requires flexibility. Nonetheless, in an effort to introduce you in a cohesive manner to the basic principles of field research, the chapters that follow present suggestions derived from generations of researchers— guidelines for you to use as a flashlight, rather than a map, throughout your journey into field research. The second theme of this guide, ethical issues in field research, is the topic of the next chapter.

Chapter Highlights

1. Field research is the systematic study of ordinary events and activities in the settings in which they occur.

2. A goal of field research is to understand what these activities and events mean to those who engage in them.

3. Interactions with participants in the setting, including observations and informal interviews, are the primary means of collecting data during field research.

4. The field researcher's experiences are recorded in the form of field notes and analyzed for a publication or final manuscript.

5. Field research is an interpretive process—researchers' interpretation of the data can be influenced by their biography and status characteristics.

6. At times, disagreement exists over some facets of what field research is, how it should be conducted, and how it should be evaluated.

7. Status characteristics affect many aspects of the field research process: What is learned during field research is not independent of who the researcher is.

Exercises

---

1. If you are going to conduct field research, you may need to include a description of field research in your proposal. Summarize, in paragraph form, what field research is on the basis of the characteristics given in this chapter.

2. Field researchers often publish their work in academic journals. Search the Internet for a Web site that provides a list of qualitative research journals. Follow the links to five journals. Browse the table of contents for several issues and read the purpose or mission statement for each journal. Summarize the differences and similarities among the five journals. For example, how do the types of articles and the audience for the journals differ? Are the journals' purposes similar?

3. Discuss the myriad ways that your college experiences are affected by your particular combination of status characteristics. Be sure to discuss both the privileges and the costs of having a particular configuration of characteristics.

2

Ethical Issues in
Qualitative Field Research

Ethical considerations permeate every aspect of the field research process, from selecting the research topic to disseminating the results. The often prolonged and personal interactions with those in the setting during field research create the possibility of myriad ethical questions, none of which are accompanied by easy solutions.

Fortunately, professional organizations recognize the ethical difficulties faced by the field researcher and have established codes designed to guide ethical decision making. With the advancements in technology, such codes are now only a mouse click away. For example, on its Web site, the American Anthropological Association (n.d.) provides the Code of Ethics established by the American Sociological Association (ASA), the American Anthropological Association, the American Political Science Association, the National Association of Social Workers, and other disciplines. It bears noting, however, that although members of the organizations are expected to adhere to their respective codes of ethics, such codes provide guidance only—not hard-and-fast rules.

To begin to sensitize you to the salience and complexity of ethical questions in fieldwork, I present in this chapter three major ethical concerns that field researchers face: **informed consent, deception,** and **confidentiality.** These three concerns are more or less relevant in different research contexts, and field researchers hold diverse ethical positions regarding them.

Let's begin our discussion of ethics with a classic example and questions to ponder. From 1965 to 1968, Laud Humphreys (1970) performed research by acting as a lookout for men who engaged in sex with other men in restrooms in public parks. Humphreys then recorded some of the men's license plate numbers and used them to obtain their names and addresses. Slightly modifying his appearance so that he would not be recognized, he interviewed some of the men at their homes, asking them questions that were part of a larger health study being conducted by another researcher. Included in this questionnaire were a few questions of particular interest to Humphreys, although none of them referred directly to the behavior of the men in the restrooms.

Clearly, Humphreys's approach raises many ethical questions, which I will use to frame this discussion on ethics. Was it ethical for Humphreys not to tell the men in the restrooms that he was a researcher gathering data? Was it ethical for him to write down their license numbers without their permission and obtain their names and addresses? Was it ethical for Humphreys not to identify himself during the health interview portion of his research, not to tell the men how they were selected to be interviewed, and not to give the men the whole truth about how some of their answers were going to be used? In order to answer such questions, one must consider the salient issues of informed consent, deception, and confidentiality.

Informed Consent

In many research contexts, ethical research on human subjects requires informed consent of the participants in the research. The ASA Code of Ethics discusses this concept in detail:

> Informed consent is a basic ethical tenet of scientific research on human populations. Sociologists do not involve a human being as a subject in research without the informed consent of the subject or the subject's legally authorized representative, except as otherwise specified in this Code. (American Sociological Association, 1999, p. 12)

The ASA code states that informed consent is required of research subjects if the "data are collected from research participants through any form of communication, interaction, or intervention" (1999, p. 12) or if the "behavior of research participants occurs in a private context where an individual can reasonably expect that no observation or reporting is taking place" (p. 12).

To obtain informed consent, the researcher must make potential participants aware of 11 pieces of information:

1. that they are participating in research

2. the purpose of the research

3. the procedures used during the research

4. the risks and benefits of the research

5. the voluntary nature of the research participation

6. their right to stop the research at any time

7. the procedures used to protect confidentiality

8. their right to have all their questions answered at any time

9. other information relevant to the participants

10. what is required of them if they consent to participate

11. that refusal to participate or withdraw at any time will lead to no foreseeable consequences (American Sociological Association, 1999, p. 13).

When discussing informed consent and in any written materials, researchers should use language that is understandable to the participants in the research. Informed consent documents are not the place to practice one's scholarly vocabulary. Only after the potential participant understands each of the items in an informed consent document and agrees to participate can the research begin.

For research that requires a great deal of involvement from the participants, such as multiple interviews and prolonged observations, **Institutional Review Boards** suggest that they be told about the research and that informed consent forms be given to them well in advance of the start of the research. This allows the potential participant to consult with others and reflect upon their willingness to participate. At the end of this section, I will provide more information about the role of Institutional Review Boards.

In some cases, the standard procedures for informed consent are not enough, and additional requirements must be met. For example, professors who want to conduct research using students in their classes have to "recognize the possibility of undue influence or subtle pressures on" students because of professors' authority over them (American Socio-logical Association, 1999, p. 12). Faculty must ensure that students face no negative consequences for declining or withdrawing from the research (p. 13). When conducting research that includes underage children, parents or legal guardians must give informed consent, and the children must give **assent**. This also applies to most college students who are 17 years old or younger.

Given the above guidelines, one could conclude that Humphreys's research was unethical. He did not obtain informed consent. The men during the observation stage did not know they were research subjects. Further, he should have allowed potential subjects days, if not weeks, to decide if they wanted to be involved given the sensitive nature and the potentially serious ramifications of being a participant in his study. However, before we label his work unethical, let's return to the ASA Code of Ethics.

The ASA allows for exceptions to the requirement of informed consent. The researcher does not have to obtain informed consent if the "research involves no more than minimal risk for research participants" and "the research could not practically be carried out were informed consent to be required" (American Sociological Association, 1999, p. 12). Although the men's answers to the health questionnaire meet the first condition of no more than minimal risk, might there have been negative implications if the men Humphreys interviewed recognized him? Some who have criticized Humphreys did so on the grounds that he should have delegated the administration of the health questionnaire to others. Indeed, he conducted only some of the health interviews with the men he observed. The observation portion of his research meets the second con-dition (not practically possible if informed consent were required) but not the first condition (no more than minimal risk). Because research must meet both conditions before an exception is given, Humphreys's study does not qualify for this exception.

Another exemption to the informed consent requirement involves research conducted in public places. The ASA code specifically lists "natu-ralistic observations in public places" (1999, p. 12) as an example of research that would not need informed consent. The code further specifies that informed consent is required if the research is in a "private context where an individual can reasonably expect that no observation or report-ing is taking place" (p. 12).

Some who defend Humphreys do so on the grounds that he was doing naturalistic observations in a "public" restroom. My own classes have participated in heated discussions trying to resolve the question of whether a public restroom in a public park is "public" or "private." Some students argue that because certain parts of the restrooms are public, no informed consent is needed; others, however, assert that because some parts are private—such as the stalls, where the user does not expect to be observed—informed consent is required.

Similar questions arise regarding the line between public and private in other settings. For example, do you need to obtain informed consent to study a conversation between two people who are whispering while awaiting their meal in a restaurant? Field researchers conduct a lot of naturalistic observations in public places, and they might even hold in-depth interviews with some individuals in the setting. The impracticality of getting informed consent from everyone who enters a setting and the generally low risk involved means that informed consent is not always required.

The issue of informed consent has other wrinkles as well. For example, the Code of Ethics requires informed consent when any recording technologies are used, including tape recording, videotaping, or filming. Even with this requirement, though, the code allows for an exception. If the activities being recorded "involve simply naturalistic observations in public places and it is not anticipated that the recording will be used in a manner that could cause personal identification or harm" (American Sociological Association, 1999, p. 14), then no informed consent is required.

Duneier's (1999) work among the book and magazine street vendors in Greenwich Village provides us with an example of recording without informed consent. From the "regular" participants and from selected interviewees, such as a woman who happened to be passing by, he obtained informed consent; however, he did not obtain it when he recorded a street vendor's interaction with a police officer. In this instance, when the officer told one of the vendors to move, Duneier discreetly turned on his tape recorder. Duneier recorded the interaction because the discussion between the officer and vendor centered on the issue of respect, a theme in his work. Because nothing occurred during this interaction that would have created potential harm for the vendor or the police officer, who was following standard procedures, informed consent was not required.

As you can tell from this brief discussion, the ASA has established clear guidelines for obtaining informed consent. However, these guidelines are insufficient when the researcher faces situations that are not specified in the code or are ambiguous.

Deception

Inextricably linked to informed consent is the issue of deception, which in research can occur in a variety of ways. For example, deception results when people are not told they are participating in a study, are misled about the purpose or details of the research, or are not aware of the correct identity or status of the researcher. If any such deception occurs during the research, then the participants do not have the opportunity to give informed consent; they simply are not fully informed.

Scholars debate about whether and when deception in a research project is acceptable. On one side of the debate rest those who assert that deception in field research is indeed acceptable. Proponents of this perspective argue that in field research informed consent is not necessary and might in fact be counterproductive. One justification offered by this group focuses on the place in which such research occurs: They argue that because it takes place in a natural setting, with little manipulation and control over the people in the setting, any potential for harm remains small. Another justification for using deception involves the belief that some types of research might be impossible without it, as was the case with the observations conducted by Humphreys. If deception had not been used, some of the men might have declined to be part of the research. Further, informed consent may lead to so much **reactivity** that the research becomes meaningless. Gans (1962) expressed this view when he wrote, "If the researcher is completely honest with people about his activities, they will try to hide actions and attitudes they consider undesirable, and so will be dishonest. Consequently, the researcher must be dishonest to get honest data" (p. 42).

Humphreys used deception in two ways. First, he did not let the men in the restroom know that he was a researcher, although they knew they were being observed. This type of research is called **covert research,** which is conducted without those in the setting being aware of the researcher's dual roles—participant and researcher. If the members in the setting are aware of the dual roles, the research is classified as **overt research.** Second, Humphreys engaged in deception when he changed his appearance for the health interview and did not let the men know at this time that he had seen them in the restroom.

Without deception, Humphreys might not have been able to conduct his research. Obtaining informed consent from the men who stopped by the restrooms would have been problematic—after all, giving consent to a stranger to be part of a research study when engaging in clandestine behavior is not likely. Additionally, those who might have given consent might not have been like the other participants. Indeed, the men who knew he was a researcher were more likely to be single and self-identify as gay men, unlike many of the other men who frequented the restrooms. If Humphreys had relied only on the men who knew he was a researcher, he would not have learned that many of the men who frequented the restrooms were heterosexual men who occasionally engaged in sex with other men.

The ASA Code of Ethics contains guidelines on deception that might help us resolve the longstanding debate about Humphreys's work. First, the code states quite simply that "[s]ociologists do not use deceptive techniques" (American Sociological Association, 1999, p. 14). The code then elaborates: "Sociologists never deceive research participants about significant aspects of the research that would affect their willingness to participate, such as physical risks, discomfort, or unpleasant emotional experiences" (p. 14). Although these statements sound like a clear mandate, the Code of Ethics allows for exceptions. Deception can be considered ethical if (a) the deception will not harm the participants, (b) the deception is justified by the study's value, (c) alternative procedures are not possible, and (d) the research has the approval of an Institutional Review Board (p. 14). If these conditions are met and deception deemed a needed feature of the research design, the code requires that sociologists "attempt to correct any misconceptions that research participants may have no later than at the conclusion of the research" (p. 14). The code gives one other exception:

> On rare occasions, sociologists may need to conceal their identities in order to undertake research that could not practicably be carried out were they to be known as researchers. Under such circumstances, sociologists undertake the research if it involves no more than minimal risk for the research participants and if they have obtained approval to proceed in this manner from an institutional review board. (p. 14)

Sometimes researchers have felt when studying powerful individuals that deception is acceptable. If deception is not allowed and informed consent is required, Galliher argues that this could prevent social scientists from uncovering "corrupt, illegitimate, covert practices of government or industry" (1982, p. 160), thereby sheltering the very communities he believes researchers have an ethical mandate to study. During his research in South Africa in the 1960s, van den Berghe expressed a similar position:

> From the outset, I decided that I should have no scruples in deceiving the government. . . . The question is, how much honor is proper for the sociologist in studying the membership and organization of what he considers an essentially dishonorable, morally outrageous, and destructive enterprise. (1968, p. 187)

More recently, Taylor and Bogdan (1998) reiterated the view that because members of a powerful group are less likely to grant permission, in order to achieve project goals, researchers studying them might have to engage in deception. An unwillingness to use deception, they argue, results in researchers exposing "the faults of the powerless while the powerful remain unscathed. To study powerful groups covertly, therefore may well be warranted morally and ethically" (p. 37). They add the compelling qualification that it is "difficult to justify outright deception of anyone merely for the sake of completing degree requirements or adding a publication in an obscure journal to a vita" (p. 37).

Deciding the appropriateness of deception requires weighing the benefits of the research against the potential risk. Although Humphreys's work was highly criticized, others viewed it as an important contribution, so much so that the book that resulted, *Tearoom Trade: Impersonal Sex in Public Places,* received the prestigious C. Wright Mills Award. This example illustrates once again the lack of a clear standard for determining the parameters of ethical research.

Regardless of what is set forth in their Code of Ethics, researchers from a variety of theoretical perspectives do not find deception acceptable. For the purposes of illustration, in the following discussions and throughout this guide, I will concentrate on a **feminist** perspective because that is the tradition within which I have been trained. However, you should note that many field researchers adhered to the same principles that I will discuss long before feminists began articulating them, and others make the same arguments without viewing them as unique to feminist researchers.

One of the first rules of medicine is *Primum non nocere,* which translates as "First, do no harm." This precept could also be one of the first rules of ethical feminist field research. Using a broad view of harm adopted by some feminists, an ethical field researcher is one who does not (a) harm anyone involved with the research, (b) harm the setting, (c) harm the researcher himself or herself, (d) harm the profession represented, or (e) harm the reciprocal relationships formed in the setting.

One premise of a feminist ethical stance is that the processes and outcomes of field research are greatly affected by the reciprocal relationships that develop between the researcher and those individuals he or she meets within the setting (Sieber, 1982). For example, the field researcher might come to share the participants' emotional pains, secrets, fears, insecurities, strengths, and accomplishments. In return, the field researcher might offer support, compassion, encouragement, advice, and even deep friendship. Participants in the setting also share and respond to the field researcher's thoughts and emotions. These reciprocal relationships form the moral basis of ethical decisions (Sieber, 1982). In sum, because researchers expect those in the setting to be honest with them, any deception on their part damages the reciprocal nature of the relationship. As a result, field research that employs deception is considered unethical.

In many cases, deceiving the members of a setting is not realistically possible and attempting to do so would immediately affect the field researcher's credibility. Although field research is possible in a setting where one is already an accepted member, this is not often the case. In most instances, the researcher is an outsider. The researcher often differs in age, social class, educational level, skin color, grooming habits, body language, religious affiliation, country of origin, customs, and worldview. Most group members will know that the researcher is new to the setting; consequently, it becomes virtually impossible to deceive them about the researcher's dual role. For example, while conducting research in Midsouth County, my midwestern accent immediately identified me as an outsider. Rather than attempt to conceal my purpose, I openly communicated my research role to most of those with whom I came into contact. For the most part, community members were flattered to be of research interest and were willing to talk, include me in events, and show me around. Not being truthful would probably have led to suspicion, resentment, and lack of cooperation—not to mention my own tension about lying to my new friends.

Another argument against deception is that, within limits, most people allow researchers some latitude in asking questions that might be deemed stupid, blunt, or nosy if they came from fellow members of the community. For example, in Midsouth County, women at the housing project under study were clearly aware of my research interest in health care issues, so it was appropriate for me to ask for information that otherwise might have been considered too personal. If my research on women's health concerns were not explicit, most likely valuable information—information that was useful to the health professionals in the area—would have been unobtainable.

In Midsouth County, my honesty about being a researcher allowed me entrée into places that otherwise might be taboo. For example, outsiders are not always welcome in Midsouth County, partly because of the history of tension and violence between the outside representatives of coal companies and local union members. When I explained my concern for women's health and my background, I was able to reduce some of their legitimate suspicion toward outsiders, and ultimately I was made to feel welcome. My status as someone who had a background of rural poverty—my home when I was growing up did not having running water or an inside toilet—was an asset in this setting. I have no illusions that I was fully trusted, but I do believe that the women I met appreciated the respect I gave them by telling them the truth about my research interests.

Confidentiality

Another important ethical issue in field research is confidentiality. One of the requirements of informed consent is to inform those in the study whether the research is anonymous, confidential, or neither. Research is **anonymous** when the researcher is not able to identify the participants in the study. In a confidential study, the researcher knows or could know the identities of the participants but does not reveal this knowledge. Sometimes research participants agree to allow disclosure of their identities. For example, when Jean Hamm (2003) conducted research on the Konnarock Training School, she not only received permission to use the women's names in her dissertation, but also included photographs of several.

A great deal of fieldwork is done under conditions of confidentiality, and for the resulting research to be considered ethical this confidentiality must be strictly guarded. Protecting confidentiality is not always as easy as it sounds. While undertaking his dissertation research on African American urban males, Nkrumah D'Angelo Lewis (2005) worried about such confidentiality issues. He interviewed men who lived in the same neighborhood and were fairly close friends. He could easily protect the identities of the men from those who did not live in the community. Yet, he struggled with finding a way to maintain the integrity of the men's comments without them being able to identify each other. His quandary was a simple one: If he reported the narrative as it was told to him, how easily could other men in the community identify the speaker?

Clearly, violating confidentiality can cause harm to members—a serious ethical violation in and of itself. In addition, researchers sometimes have to withhold other sensitive information. For example, some of my colleagues and I were conducting research in Midsouth County with members of a grassroots organization who told us that they had secretly hired a water expert to determine whether their drinking water was safe. They did not want the water board to know that they were independently testing the water. If we leaked their plans, the water board might have made temporary adjustments to make it look as if the water was safe when it was not. Had we disclosed this information before the tests were completed, we could have seriously damaged the group's endeavors to improve drinking water quality.

Another example from Midsouth County involved the admission by some health care professionals that they occasionally lied on government forms in order to help their clients receive needed medical care for low or no costs. Although I think they should be commended for their humanitarian efforts, it is likely that neither their supervisors nor government officials would have found their practices laudable.

Maintaining confidentiality becomes particularly problematic when authorities think the researcher has knowledge that a law has been violated. This was the case for Rik Scarce (1994) when he was a graduate student performing research on animal liberation activists. In an attempt to obtain information about a suspect in a raid on a laboratory at Washington State University, authorities contacted him. Committed to the confidentiality agreements he had given the participants, Scarce refused to reveal to a federal grand jury the names of those he interviewed or the context of any interviews. As a result, he spent 159 days in jail.

Scarce's decision not to break confidentiality is consistent with the ASA Code of Ethics. The code states that researchers have "an obligation to ensure that confidential information is protected" and that researchers should "take reasonable precautions to protect the confidentiality rights of the research participants" (American Sociological Association, 1999, p. 9). The code does not provide an exception for legal pressures to disclose information:

> Confidential information provided by research participants . . . is treated as such by sociologists even if there is no legal protection or privilege to do so. Sociologists have an obligation to protect confidential

information and not allow information gained in confidence from being used in ways that would unfairly compromise research participants. (p. 9)

The Code of Ethics indicates that researchers need to "inform themselves fully about all the laws and rules that may limit or alter guarantees of confidentiality" (American Sociological Association, 1999, p. 10). For example, confidentiality cannot be broken even after the death of the participant.

The Code of Ethics also indicates that researchers must determine their ability to guarantee absolute confidentiality and inform participants of any limitations. I suggest that if you think keeping the identities of the research participants confidential might be problematic—ethically, legally, morally, socially, or physically—then it is best not to undertake the research. For example, let's pretend that you would like to do research on the role of club drugs, such as Ecstasy, at raves. Yet, you know you would sing like a bird if authorities asked you who you saw using drugs. The code states that you should either (a) not do the research or (b) indicate clearly on the informed consent and discuss thoroughly with participants that if faced with legal threat, you will break confidentiality. Only if they are willing to accept the limited confidentiality agreement that you are offering them could research begin.

Confidentiality can be broken under some circumstances, but the researcher should do so only after careful consideration. For example, if you become aware that the participant's life is in danger or the welfare of a child is at risk, then promises of confidentiality should be ignored. The circumstances under which you would break confidentiality should be included on the informed consent. Unfortunately, the dilemma of whether to break confidentiality is usually prompted by conditions considerably more complicated than the two examples presented here.

Sometimes researchers get into situations where they believe they have a moral and legal duty to violate confidentiality, although as researchers they have promised not to do so. For example, in his ethnographic study of a U.S. police department, Van Maanen (1982) reported the following incident in which two police officers, Barns and McGee, throw a suspect, Blazier, into a police van. Van Maanen wrote,

> From outside the van I can hear the distinct smack of wood meeting flesh and bone. After perhaps a half minute or so, Blazier, thoroughly dazed and maybe unconscious, is pulled from the wagon, bounced to

the pavement, handcuffed, and tossed back in . . . In the prowl car, Barns remarks: "What a place to try to put somebody out. It's so f___ing cramped and dark in the van you don't know what's going on. I kept hitting something with my stick, but I didn't know what it was until I heard the creep's glasses shatter. Then I kept hitting the same spot unit I felt it got kind of squishy" . . . This episode was neither the most violent nor the most blatantly questionable police incident I have observed in the course of my studies. (p. 137)

Barns and McGee know that Van Maanen is a researcher. They also know that they had been promised confidentiality. However, a man's life is possibly at stake. The police officers may have broken laws. Should Van Maanen report this incident? If he does, he will probably not be able to continue his research. Is documenting the brutality and publishing the results more important than this one incident? Should he have tried to intervene at the time of the incident? No easy answers to these questions exist.

Like Scarce, Van Maanen (1982) later was subpoenaed to testify and turn over his field notes on the Blazier incident. Van Maanen attended the hearing as required but refused either to testify or submit his notes. Shortly thereafter, the case was dropped, sparing Van Maanen the kind of decision Scarce had to make.

Part of the debate regarding confidentiality revolves around issues of power—the power of those doing the harm versus those being harmed. Some argue that it is unethical to break the confidentiality of the relatively powerless—such as prostitutes, factory workers, and poor people—but not so to break agreements with powerful groups or institutions acting as oppressors of such individuals. Bulmer (1982) took this position when he wrote,

> Specifically social scientists are seen as having a responsibility to study those institutions or government agencies that are in a position to mistreat the disadvantaged, and if evidence of wrongdoing is discovered on the part of government officials or administrators, it should be publicly disclosed in an effort to discourage future wrongdoings—regardless of any promises made to the public officials to respect confidential information. (p. 21)

Think about the Blazier case. Blazier was a relatively powerless man who was beaten by powerful agents of social control. Using Bulmer's arguments, Van Maanen had an ethical duty to break his promise of confidentiality to the police.

In contrast, others argue that status characteristics—such as the amount of power individuals possess—should not be a consideration in ethical decisions. According to this school of thought, everyone should be treated equally. However, in practice this is a difficult position to maintain—and not everyone agrees that it is a desirable goal.

Let's use the Blazier example again to see if the tenet of treating everyone equally proves easy to follow. How important is the confidentiality of the police officers if Blazier is a murderer who got off on a technicality? If Blazier is an old man with a drinking problem? If Blazier is the son of the governor of your state? If Blazier is one of your college friends? If Blazier is your father? What if the police officers are your friends or relatives?

Another argument against breaking confidentiality even in cases that involve the researcher's knowledge of wrongdoing is that if this practice became the standard, research would become harder to accomplish. Access to the very businesses, organizations, individuals, and institutions that Bulmer (1982) and Taylor and Bogdan (1998) say we have a responsibility to study would be denied.

Luckily, maintaining confidentiality is not always a problem, because it is not always required. The Code of Ethics states: "Confidentiality is not required with respect to observations in public places, activities conducted in public, or other settings where no rules of privacy are provided by law or custom. Similarly, confidentiality is not required in the case of information available from public records" (American Sociological Association, 1999, p. 10). The lack of confidentiality and informed consent requirements make field research conducted in public places ideal for students who have been assigned a class project.

If you are planning on conducting field research, you will have to address many ethical questions, such as the following:

1. Is informed consent required?

2. If so, who in the setting will receive the informed consent?

3. What will be included in the informed consent?

4. Will the research be covert and include deception to prevent reactivity?

5. How will the confidentiality of the participants in the setting be protected?

Fortunately, prior to beginning your research, you will have opportunities to ask for and receive help resolving some of these ethical decisions. Certainly, consultation with your professor or major advisor will provide excellent guidance. Then, in most cases, you will have to submit appropriate materials to an Institutional Review Board for approval, which is necessary for ethical research on human subjects and required by most colleges and universities.

Institutional Review Board

Prior to undertaking a project involving human subjects, a researcher must seek Institutional Review Board (IRB) approval. At that time, he or she can request an exemption, an expedited review, or a full review by the board. Essentially, the more complex the project, the more complex the approval process. An exemption might be granted for field research taking place in a public place with only minimal risk to participants. For example, if you conducted a simple field research study in a local coffee shop, you would most likely be granted an exemption from the requirement of informed consent. However, if you decided to tape-record interviews with individuals at the coffee shop—a process that demands considerably more involvement from participants—your project would be the subject of an expedited review, and ultimately you would be required to request informed consent. Research at a group home for juvenile delinquents would require a full review by the IRB, and chances are good that as a student you would not be given permission to undertake such a project. In fact, even your professor would be allowed to perform this research only after all sorts of safeguards were in place, since young people with criminal records who are under confinement are considered a special class needing extra protection.

If you are an undergraduate student conducting research for a class, your instructor will provide information about the IRB policies that apply to you. If you are a graduate student doing research on human subjects for your thesis or dissertation, you will need to seek IRB approval.

Just as there are divergent views about what field research is, how it should be conducted, when it was first undertaken, and how it should be evaluated, there are also divergent views regarding what makes—or does not make—research ethical. Because of the complexity and importance of ethics in field research, this theme will be embedded throughout this guide.

Chapter Highlights
---

1. Ethical concerns in field research are often present and usually complex.

2. Not all field researchers agree on what is deemed unethical during field research.

3. Codes of ethics developed by different disciplines provide guidelines for making ethical decisions.

4. Research can be overt or covert—with covert research being ethical only under limited conditions.

5. The reciprocal relationship between the researcher and members of the setting is considered when making ethical decisions.

6. Informed consent is usually necessary when the research is more than observations in public places.

7. Ethical research requires that no harm be done to members of the setting, to the researcher, to the profession, or to the relationship between the researcher and the members in the setting.

8. Keeping promises of confidentiality can at times be difficult for the field researcher.

Exercises
---

1.   Imagine that you are conducting field research on a high school program that is designed to help students at risk of dropping out of high school. This program is not particularly well received by the community, but your research is showing that the program is effective. In the course of your research, you discover that one of several counselors for this program is sexually harassing some of the students. You have promised confidentiality. Should you tell anyone? If yes, when? If no, why not? What would the ASA Code of Ethics recommend that you do? Be sure to discuss the implications of the decisions that you make (Fetterman, 1982).

2.   Reread the section recounting the Blazier incident. As an ethical researcher, what would you do if you observed this interaction? Is your answer affected by Blazier's status characteristics? Is your answer affected by your status characteristics? Is your answer affected by the purpose of your research? Consider whether your decision would vary under the following conditions:
   a.   You are conducting the research for a class project.
   b.   You were hired by the police to do the research.

  c. You were hired by the ACLU to do the research.

  d. You are engaging in the research because you have a professional interest in the topic, and you hope that a publication will result from it.

3. John Van Maanen (1982) reported on an incident in which the police threw a boy of approximately 10 years of age to the pavement and verbally assaulted him because the child "had aimed a ceremonial upright third finger in the direction of the passing patrol car" (p. 137). Van Maanen felt that the police reacted as they did partly because of his presence in the car. Discuss the ethical issues involved in this incident and possible ways of responding.

4. The National Cancer Institute offers online training in the ethical treatment of human subjects. Link to http://cme.cancer.gov/clinicaltrials/learning/human participant-protections.asp and take the course. When finished, you will receive a certificate of completion.

5. The National Institutes of Health now makes available a Certificate of Confidentiality. Link to http://grants1.nih.gov/grants/policy/coc/index.htm. Summarize the purposes of and procedures for obtaining the certificate. Indicate what protections are afforded and how long they are in effect. Include in your answer what is meant by sensitive information for the purposes of the certificate.

3

Prelude to Qualitative Fieldwork

Now that you have received a broad overview of field research and gained an awareness of some of its ethical concerns, you are ready to learn specific details about planning a field research project. To that end, I provide suggestions for selecting a research topic, creating preliminary goals and research questions, reviewing the literature, and making final preparations.

Selecting a Research Topic

Researchers usually decide to conduct field research because they believe it is the best way to examine a particular setting, group, and social processes and structures that are of interest to them theoretically, personally, or academically. Fieldwork allows them to effectively seek in-depth answers, based on the perspectives of those in the setting, to research questions that intrigue them.

Examples of projects undertaken by field researchers can illustrate the range of interests of scholars who engage in field research and possibly help generate ideas for those of you who are required to undertake fieldwork as a class assignment. Among the topics that have been the focus of published field research one finds

- the Maya Biosphere Reserve in Guatemala (Sundberg, 2004);
- the wives of professional athletes (Ortiz, 2004);
- genital piercing, branding, burning, and cutting (Myers, 1994);

- two Native American social movement organizations challenging educational practices (Gongaware, 2003);
- pregnant women's under-utilization of clinic-based prenatal services in Mozambique (Chapman, 2003);
- a food bank that distributes food to the needy in southern Canada (Tarasuk & Eakin, 2003);
- women farmers in central Pennsylvania (Trauger, 2004);
- a symphony orchestra in Soka Gakkai, Japan (Levi, 2003).

Of course, this list focuses on projects undertaken by professional, practicing field researchers, and as such it presents ideas that are at times grand and far-reaching in scope, even international in focus. If you are assigned a research project in a college course in the United States of America, you are not going to be expected to study a symphony orchestra in Japan or clinic-based prenatal services in Mozambique. As a student, you will be pleased to know that your local community can offer rich resources for a field research project. Consider some of the topics students in my classes have studied:

- employees at a local sewage treatment facility,
- a church where members handle snakes as part of their religious rituals,
- a rural grocery store where dances are held on Friday nights,
- the process of selecting a pet at an animal shelter,
- gendered interactions among sky divers.

In addition, my students have conducted field research in the university library, dorm cafeterias, more than a few local bars, and other settings familiar to college students.

Several factors influence the selection of the final project. For example, a researcher must consider how much of a time investment a particular topic will take. The choice is often affected by the scholar's theoretical perspective and area of expertise. Curiosity about and availability of a social group or setting are motivating factors.

The status characteristics of researchers and their values also can influence project selection. For example, Bourgois (1995) explains how economic, theoretical, personal, and political perspectives motivated his research:

> When I first moved to East Harlem—'El Barrio'—as a newlywed in the spring of 1985, I was looking for an inexpensive New York City apartment from which I could write a book on the experience of poverty and

ethnic segregation in the heart of one of the most expensive cities in the world. On the level of theory, I was interested in the political economy of inner-city street culture. From a personal, political perspective, I wanted to probe the Achilles heel of the richest industrialized nation in the world by documenting how it imposes racial segregation and economic marginalization on so many of its Latino/a and African-American citizens. (p. 1)

Whereas researchers often possess years of training within a particular field and have a well-defined theoretical orientation, both of which assist them in the selection of research topics, not all of you will have these advantages. Nonetheless, you most likely have a worldview of some sort and, hopefully, you will have some disciplinary interests to help decide what topic you want to explore.

Once you have determined whether you will focus your research project on a particular setting or on a selected social group, you can then turn your attention to one of the themes introduced earlier in this guide: ethical considerations.

Ethical Issues

One goal of your selection process is to focus on projects that are ethically well grounded. Although you cannot predict all of the ethical issues that could possibly arise from your choice of a field research project, you can minimize such problems by asking yourself a series of questions before finalizing where you will do your research. First, can the research you are considering be completed without deception? Deception is tempting when you think that participants in the setting will change their behavior enough to make the research meaningless as a result of your presence. If you think this will be the case, in order to avoid slipping into deceptive practices, you should probably select another project. Second, how difficult will it be to keep promises of confidentiality? As discussed earlier, confidentiality issues are more problematic during research on illegal, immoral, or unethical behaviors. Third, what are your chances of getting **dirty hands** while conducting this research—of participating in illegal behavior or behavior that is against your own moral standards? You need to be particularly careful about illegal behaviors because engaging in research cannot be used as a legal defense for breaking the law.

Fourth, what are the chances that your research will harm someone in the setting? Even if you maintain confidentiality, can your presence in the setting be distressful to group members? For instance, if you decide to study mothers receiving Temporary Aid to Needy Families, would your research interest in them make these mothers feel somehow unfit or different in spite of your reassurance to the contrary? Might your final report bring unintended, negative consequences to group members?

Finally, could the project be harmful to your personal safety? Do the responses of others to your race, ethnicity, gender, age, or sexual orientation put you at risk? Simply being an outsider can increase your risk in some situations. For example, Maria Macabuac (2005) elected to conduct her dissertation research in the Philippines. She had already written her proposal and received approval from her committee, but just as she was about to undertake the fieldwork portion of her research, violence in the area she wanted to study increased considerably. Although she is from the Philippines, Macabuac's ethnic status made it unsafe for her to be in the region where she planned to collect her data. With prodding and approval from her committee, she selected another site, a decision that required modification of her focus and a delay in her data collection. As is often the case when field researchers have to deviate from their original design, the adjustments Macabuac made in her project resulted in an excellent dissertation.

These questions cover just a few of the ethical issues you should ponder as you begin the process of selecting a field research project. As with most aspects of field research, there is no complete list of ethical issues to consider—nor is there a rulebook on how to resolve ethical issues in project selection.

At this point in your determination of a research topic, you can now turn your attention to practical issues.

Practicality

There are numerous practical issues to consider in selecting a research topic. One important issue is time. Field research requires long-term engagement with those being studied. Do you have enough time to commit to a project that interests you? Do you have the flexibility to make observations during different times of day and night? How long fieldwork takes varies greatly from project to project, but be warned that however long you think your particular project will take is probably an underestimation of the time you will actually need. Keep in mind that even fairly narrowly defined projects undertaken by seasoned field researchers can take years to complete. Graduate students often need to consider whether their research can be completed before their funding runs out.

Think about your interpersonal skills as you go about selecting your research setting. If you are extremely shy, you might want to avoid settings where interacting with strangers would be a frequent requirement. Field research is not for the fainthearted. Even a place as familiar as a car dealership can feel alien when one is there to conduct field research. For example, in speaking of her experiences with women sales agents, Helene Lawson (2000) noted that "I felt, much as other field workers before me, unfamiliar with the social world under investigation and a resulting sense of edginess, uncertainty, discomfort, and anxiety" (p. 135).

Regardless of this warning, you need not always avoid settings in which you might feel ill at ease. Researchers who are not only uncomfortable but also downright miserable in a setting have done wonderful research. Eleanor Miller (1986), for instance, wrote that overcoming her fear was part of her motivation to continue her research on women involved in crime. However, your primary goal is to complete the research, and you simply won't be able to finish it if you end up in a setting that requires more investment in resources than you are willing or able to give.

Accessibility

Another important question in topic selection is access. Sites range from open—requiring no permission to enter—to closed—requiring permission to enter. Most public areas such as local parks, swimming pools, and libraries are open. You do not have to obtain permission to be there, although you still need to decide whether your research will be overt or covert and whether informed consent is required. At the other extreme are closed private settings, such as homes. Some settings, such as elementary schools, are for security reasons governed by laws and regulations restricting access. Even when channels are available for obtaining permission, following the necessary procedures for gaining access can increase the time required to complete the research.

Often, field researchers discover that they are not allowed in a particular setting because of their status characteristics. If you are of the "wrong" gender, for example, you might be denied access to numerous activities, roles, and locations designated as appropriate for only one gender (Warren, 1988). Restrictions can also be based on other status characteristics such as age, sexual orientation, race, ethnicity, or religion.

Even if you can gain access to a setting, those within it might restrict your observations and interactions as a result of your status characteristics. For example, if you were doing field research on members of The Church of Jesus Christ of Latter-day Saints, you would not be able to observe some religious rituals unless you were a member of this church. Sometimes a combination of status characteristics is used to restrict access. For example, because Peggy Golde (1986) was a woman, she was not accepted in the world of men during her study of the Nahua Indians of Mexico. In addition, the fact that she was unmarried and childless also prevented her from being fully accepted into the world of the adult women. Because so many settings impose unexpected restrictions on the sorts of information you might be able to gather or observe firsthand, is it therefore better to choose a setting where you already have access?

The Familiar Versus the Unfamiliar

Whether to undertake research in a place where one is familiar is one of the most common questions students ask me when they are considering conducting field research. Opinions are mixed on whether it is better to conduct field research in a familiar or an unfamiliar setting. Some argue that if a person already understands the dynamics of a setting from the participants' perspectives, then there is little need to undertake the research. Moreover, research in unfamiliar settings might be more fruitful than research conducted in familiar ones, some claim, because cultural and social events in unfamiliar settings are easier to see (Neuman, 1991, p. 344).

Others argue that familiarity with a setting or group provides a firm foundation on which to build. Those who are familiar with a setting may already have rapport with participants, understand the nuances of language and behavioral expectations, and possess analytic insights into the working of the setting. In some instances, the only person who has a chance of being allowed to conduct research is someone who is already known to the group. This was the case for Columbus Hopper and Johnny Moore (1994), who studied women in outlaw motorcycle gangs.

Prior to the work of Hopper and Moore (1994), women's involvement in motorcycle gangs was virtually ignored. Hopper and Moore's study provided details about the place of women in biker culture, the rituals in which they engage, their role as moneymakers, and their motivations and backgrounds. Hopper and Moore were able to conduct this study only because this was a familiar setting. They write:

The main reason we were able to make contacts with bikers was the background of Johnny Moore, who was once a biker himself. During the 1960s, "Big John" was president of Satan's Dead, an outlaw club on the Mississippi Gulf Coast. He participated in the rituals we describe, and his own experience and observations provided the details of initiation ceremonies that we related. As a former club president, Moore was able to get permission for us to visit biker clubhouses, a rare privilege for outsiders. (p. 391)

An important contribution to our understanding of women's participation in motorcycle gangs would have been lost had Hopper and Moore followed the advice not to study familiar settings.

Knowing the local culture can also help facilitate the interviewing process. For example, Lewis (2005) was fortunate to know the local expectations before he began interviewing participants with a history of violence for his dissertation on interactions among African American urban men. Lewis describes the events leading up to an interview with one of the men:

Chip had just purchased his first house, to which I had been on one previous occasion. I called him from outside out of respect for his home, even though we had arranged the meeting. This is another unspoken rule. You DO NOT just "pop up" at someone's residence without giving him notice. I could tell that Chip appreciated the phone call. He said, "oh, you outside, give me a second." I waited in my jeep until the door opened about three minutes subsequent to the cessation of the phone call. (p. 74)

I believe the field research process can be more exciting if one engages in research in an unfamiliar setting. In fact, I encourage my undergraduate students to push themselves to do research in places that are foreign to them. In contrast, I advise graduate students to conduct research in places or among groups where questions of theoretical interest to them can be answered, regardless of the level of familiarity.

Record Keeping

In this chapter, I have spent considerable time discussing the process of project selection because it is not an antecedent to field research but rather an integral part of it. Why, how, and where you select a particular setting or social group will affect everything that follows. Your thoughts about where you want to conduct research, the early questions you have, your first impressions, why you reject one setting for another, and the initial contacts you make as you consider places all have implications for your work. Thus, well before any actual fieldwork begins, you should start keeping records of your activities and thoughts. As you will learn in the last chapter, a **dependability audit**—reviewing records of everything done during the research—is one of the things used to assess the quality of your research. It is at this point in the research that you begin creating such a paper trail.

In addition to keeping records of your activities during every stage of the research, you should periodically review your notes to help you plan what to do next. For example, when she began her dissertation, Chenault (2004) had only a vague idea about what she wanted to accomplish with her research in a public housing community. She had conducted mediations in the community, so she felt that she would have a certain level of access. Beyond that, she was unsure what the focus of her research might be. After receiving Institutional Review Board approval, she began talking to managers in several communities to see if that would help her generate ideas. Rather than wait to start her field notes until she was certain of her research questions, she correctly started writing them during her decision-making process. The following excerpt from her field notes represents an informal conversation with Tyler, a manager in one of the communities, during the time when she was still generating ideas for her dissertation research:

> While Tyler provided useful information regarding several areas of investigation, he repeatedly returned our conversation to the topic of "site-based meetings," saying such things as the following:
> "At site-based meetings. . . . you know and see what our community wants."
> "Site-based means everything is done."
> "Site-based meetings have full control over our properties."
> "You need to come to a site-based meeting."
>
> That man gave me a headache, I didn't get the response I wanted, and he kept talking about site-based meetings. Almost every other word was site-based meetings. I asked about a shooting death that happened in the community and he talked about the resident council. (Chenault, 2004, pp. 7–8)

You should not be surprised to learn that, after reading her field notes a few days later, she followed Tyler's lead and decided to explore the site-based meetings about which he was so enthusiastic. After attending several such meetings, she became interested in the resident council who also attended these meetings. Ultimately, the resident council became the focus of her study. In the process of reviewing a discussion captured by field notes—recorded well before she had settled upon a particular focus—she was led to explore a group that she might have overlooked otherwise. Once she had settled on a topic, she could then proceed to establishing research goals and questions.

Goals and Research Questions

Almost all field researchers have the same general purpose: to understand social interactions within the setting or social group from the perspective of the participants. In addition to this desire to understand daily life, researchers usually enter the field with general goals and a series of research questions specific to their study. Without at least some preliminary research questions, field researchers would be almost overwhelmed with the task of observing everything and talking to everyone. It is not uncommon for researchers to devise research questions *before* they have uncovered an appropriate setting for answering them. They then tailor their general research questions to the specific setting once they have decided where to conduct their fieldwork.

Sometimes field researchers begin with general goals for their research. For instance, when Robert Prus and Styllianoss Irini (1988) studied the daily lives of members of a hotel community—hookers, strippers, bartenders, cocktail waitresses, bouncers, desk clerks, bar patrons, and rounders—they began not with specific research questions, but with three simple goals. First, they wanted to understand the interrelatedness of these different groups. Second, they wanted to understand how individuals in the groups managed their careers. Third, they were interested in the interpersonal relationships in the hotel setting—such as friendships, loneliness, sexuality, and violence. It took these two researchers over three years before they felt that they had answered their questions or reached their goals sufficiently. It is difficult to guess how long their research would have taken had they established more than three goals.

Research questions in fieldwork often are formulated around "what" and "how." Since writing research questions is one of the most difficult and important components of field research, I will provide numerous examples that will help guide your own formulation of such questions.

Early in her book about homeless women, for example, Russell (1991) provides her readers with her goal and research questions. Russell indicated that she was interested in "To what extent homeless women have developed a specific culture or subculture" (p. 4). From this general goal she created a list of specific questions to provide focus for her study:

> Once a woman was without permanent shelter, what strategies did she use to survive? Where did a woman find food? What arrangements did she make for shelter? Where did she obtain clothing? Where did she bathe and launder her clothing? How and where did she fill the hours of her days? What possessions did she take with her when she became homeless? How did she view the agencies with whom she came in contact? How did she view herself and other homeless women? What were her hopes, fears, and dreams? What attitudes did she bring with her from the mainstream, and what attitudes did she change? (p. 4)

Similarly, in her study of women who sold cars, Lawson (2000) devised clear questions. How did women accomplish their careers in commission car sales? What attracted women to this occupation? What obstacles did they face as they pursued their careers (p. x)?

Duneier's (1999) study of life on the sidewalks of Sixth Avenue in Greenwich Village was based on a series of research questions. In addition to asking the basic question of how the sidewalk life works today, he also wanted to know:

> How do these persons live in a moral order? How do they have the ingenuity to do so in the face of exclusion and stigmatization on the basis of race and class? How does the way they do so affront the sensibilities of the working and middle classes? How do their acts intersect with a city's mechanisms to regulate its public spaces? (p. 9)

Researchers sometimes change their goals and research questions as their studies progress. Elliot Liebow (1994) changed his goals during the course of his research. As he began analyzing his field notes, he realized that he had discovered a new aim for his study of homeless women. Liebow explains this change early in his book:

Tell Them Who I Am focuses on the dynamics of shelter life. Initially, my aim was to write a straightforward description of shelter life and, ideally, to try to see the world of homelessness as homeless women see and experience it. Later, when trying to make sense of my notes, I realize that another of my aims was to explain both to others and myself how these women remained human in the face of inhuman conditions. (p. 1)

Similarly, Bourgois found the focus of his research in East Harlem ("El Barrio") changing from the entire underground (untaxed) economy to a focus on crack, a drug that he did not know about before 1985, when he began his five-year study (1995, p. 1).

I do not mean to imply that researchers change their goals and questions most of the time. In fact, changing one's goals or questions is particularly problematic if one already has committee and IRB approval. However, being able to revise one's research questions as one proceeds is an advantage of field research over many other methodologies. You may recall from the first chapter that flexibility is one of the key features of such research. Nonetheless, the savvy field researcher will delineate some measure of goals or questions, no matter how minimal, at the beginning of the research project.

Review of Literature

Placing one's own work into the wider context of academic literature is an important part of conducting research. I suggest that you learn about a setting by thoroughly reviewing the literature before entering the field and that you continue reading relevant literature throughout the research process. When looking for relevant literature, I advise reading field research by others who have studied your particular, or a similar, setting or group. I hope that you are already familiar with reviewing academic literature, so I will not provide detailed instructions here. However, I do suggest that in addition to academic books and articles you read newspapers, autobiographies, and historical accounts. Even novels can be useful in helping prepare you emotionally, physically, and intellectually for field research in a particular setting. Having read a wide range of literature facilitates the analysis process, as does having a good theoretical foundation.

At this point in the field research process, you probably have not spent much time—if any at all—in the actual field. You have devoted yourself to necessary prep work: determining the topic and setting, devising research goals and questions, beginning your record keeping, firmly grounding yourself in the body of existing literature. Now, you need to prepare to take your project to the next level: the field itself.

Final Preparations

When explaining to students the importance of preparing for the field, I use as an example Herbie Goldfarb, one of the characters in the book *The Milagro Beanfield War* (Nichols, 1974). Herbie arrived in Milagro as a VISTA volunteer without sufficiently preparing for the task: He did not speak Spanish (the language of Milagro); he failed to bring warm clothes because he thought the Southwest would be hot all the time (there are snowcapped mountains in the Southwest); and he shared a one-room "house" with snakes, skunks, and black widow spiders because he thought living arrangements had been made for him (they hadn't). In order to avoid becoming a Herbie Goldfarb during your field research, you need to prepare.

Conducting fieldwork in a culture or subculture extremely different from your own requires levels of preparation beyond what, because of space restrictions, this book can cover. However, one suggestion for preparation is worth mentioning. Having a contact person in the place you plan to conduct your fieldwork is priceless. Although you might be brave and adventurous enough simply to show up in a location where you do not speak the language and have made no advance plans, your field-work will be exponentially more difficult should you choose this route.

Conducting fieldwork closer to your home requires less advance preparation but still demands some measure of planning. Preparation might be something as simple as wearing appropriate clothing. Consider as well how you will record your observations and interviews. Although you might have to rely on writing field notes during observations and informal interviews, field researchers often choose to use tape recorders to capture all of the nuances of formal interviews.

In order to illustrate the differences between taking notes during interviews and tape recording, I often ask graduate students to conduct hour-long mock interviews, during which they take notes for a half-hour and then tape the last half-hour. Even when they thought they were doing a capable job of taking notes by hand, they are often embarrassed by how sparse their notes are in comparison to what was captured by the tape. In both cases, however, they are dismayed by how long it takes to transcribe the interviews. Clearly, tape recordings are far superior to hand-written notes; however, as a field researcher you must be prepared for the occasion when recording is not possible.

When you have the opportunity to tape-record interviews, I cannot stress enough the importance of having multiple tapes and batteries. You might consider having more than one tape recorder. Out of 17 students who attempted to tape interviews as part of a class requirement, four could not do so because of problems with their recorders. Several others found that external noises or the misplacement of a microphone rendered their tapes almost useless. Some researchers recommend recorders with clip-on microphones for both the interviewer and interviewee. I have become a fan of digital recorders. Even when you believe that you will be taping, also be prepared to take notes. Technology is wonderful, but it sometimes fails, and on occasion a participant will consent to being interviewed but not recorded.

A last note about preparation. Be aware that Murphy's Law frequently operates in field research: If something can go wrong, it probably will. One common problem is the "no show" interviewee. During her dissertation research in the Philippines, Mary Janet Arnado (2002) frequently encountered this problem. She made plans to interview domestic maids on their days off, but many times the women simply did not show up as planned. Arnado would reschedule and the result would be the same. Sometimes her perseverance paid off and the interview was held; at other times, her efforts proved fruitless.

Field researchers know they must prepare themselves mentally for things to go wrong. They must be willing to be flexible, to adjust, and to make compromises in their original plans. Field researchers benefit by subscribing to the German expression "Glück im Unglück," which roughly translates to "fortune in misfortune." A good researcher can turn unfortunate events into advantages.

For instance, Thomas Parkhill was able to do just this. The original goal of his research was to get to the town of Ramnagar in India so that he could study the *Ramlila,* an important religious event. Parkhill never made it to Ramnagar. Parkhill writes,

> Arriving in Banaras in early autumn, 1984, I intended to follow other scholars from the West across the Ganges River to study the Ramnagar *Ramlila,* a religious drama of widespread reputation. Determined to learn how a religious story was treated in a performance context, I spent the first days of the *Ramlila* season negotiating the river currents and the sometimes soggy Ramnagar geography. One afternoon, after I'd literally missed the boat to Ramnagar, I began to explore my own neighborhood and discovered a *Ramlila* there. (1993, p. 103)

By focusing on smaller neighborhoods, he was able to accomplish a wonderful study of the *Ramlila*. This does not mean, however, that his study was without further complications. Although he was able to visit 14 *Ramlilas*, many of them up to four times, his observations ended abruptly when the *Ramlila* season was cut short by the assassination of Indira Gandhi on October 31, 1984.

I am pointing out some of these small and not so small practical issues because they affect field research in ways they might not affect other types of research. If you get cold or hungry and your feet hurt while you are sitting at your computer doing multiple regression with variables from a national data set, you can simply stop, put on a sweater, grab a snack, and kick off your shoes. The data will still be there, and it will remain unchanged. If, however, you leave the room, the building, or the street when doing observations to get a jacket or because you are hungry and your feet hurt, things will not be the same when you return, and you will not know what happened in the meantime. If you are so overcome with insecurities and frustration that you hide in your room rather than interact with the participants in the setting, then you are not conducting fieldwork. Field research is time sensitive—the data unfold in real time. If you are not there as the research instrument to see it, gather it, or hear it, it moves on without you. Being prepared will help you be part of the experience.

Chapter Highlights

1. Numerous factors, such as theoretical importance, curiosity, time, and values, affect the selection of a research project.

2. Myriad ethical issues should be factored into the decision-making process when considering different research topics.

3. Research projects will fail or be considerably more difficult if the researcher is insufficiently prepared for the task.

4. Scholars debate whether being familiar or unfamiliar with a research site is an advantage.

5. Immediately upon considering field research, researchers should keep written records of their decisions, thoughts, and experiences related to the research.

6. Field research is guided by overarching goals and research questions.

7. Research questions are often formatted around "how" and "what" questions.

8. Situating one's research in a larger body of academic literature is a requirement of field research.

Exercises

1. Create three research questions that could guide field research on a particular setting or social group of interest to you.

2. Take notes as you conduct a 10-minute interview with a friend on a topic that requires him or her to talk at length. For example, ask about childhood or high school experiences. Transcribe the notes and describe the process. Was it easy for you to take notes and listen? Were you able to write fast enough to get most of what was said? Did note-taking affect the speed at which your friend talked? How long did it take you to transcribe the notes? Did you recall and add things as you typed? Were you able to make sense out of all your notes? Summarize your views on the benefits and costs of taking notes.

3. Locate five academic articles that employ field research, ethnography, or participant observation as the methodology. Summarize the topic of each and list the related research questions.

4. Pretend that you are an instructor for a research methods class. A student wants to conduct field research on a campus group whose purpose is to work for the legalization of marijuana. Discuss with this student all the pro and con factors that should be considered during selection of this group as a project setting.

4

The Infrastructure of
Qualitative Field Research

One of the difficulties inherent to writing about field research involves deciding how to organize the presentation of the interrelated "pieces" in order to enhance learning. This difficulty stems, in part, from the fact that qualitative researchers cannot agree on how many "pieces" exist—or even what they should be called. That different names are sometimes used to describe the same component of research adds to the confusion. However, in spite of a lack of consistency from researcher to researcher, we generally agree that all components or "pieces" are interrelated and influence each other—some in unidirectional and others in reciprocal ways. Additionally, most researchers agree that the field researcher does not proceed through steps one after the other but instead works on several parts simultaneously.

For heuristic reasons, I will use seven topics to frame this discussion: (1) **paradigms**, (2) **theory**, (3) **tradition of inquiry**, (4) **methodology**, (5) **methods**, (6) **data analysis**, and (7) **final manuscript**. Qualitative researchers work within paradigms, use theories, conduct research consistent with traditions of inquiry, design the methodological structures of their research, employ methods to collect data, perform data analysis, and write final manuscripts. More often than not, they perform some of these activities at the same time. Issues related to ethics and status characteristics also are embedded in each "piece."

Paradigms

At the time that I began writing this chapter, I learned that singer/song-writer Ani DiFranco was scheduled to appear at a music festival in nearby Floyd, an extremely small town in rural Virginia. Not knowing who she was, I browsed some of DiFranco's CDs. One of the first songs I noticed was called "Paradigm" (2005). Although I did not quite interpret this as a sign from a muse, I couldn't help checking out the lyrics to this song, as well as those to other ones by her. I was pleased to find snippets of her songs that I think are relevant to an understanding of different paradigms. (My apologies to DiFranco if I have misrepresented her views in the following discussion, which is designed to help you learn the importance of paradigms to the research process.)

Researchers' paradigmatic beliefs influence the purposes of their research, how they will conduct the research, how they will assess the role of values and ethics in their work, how they will formulate relationships to participants in the setting, how their work will be presented, and many other aspects of the research process. Because paradigms provide crucial guides to the research process, I think it important to provide an overview of them—albeit, because of space limitations, a brief and simplified one. I suggest that readers who wish to learn more about paradigms begin their quest with *The Handbook of Qualitative Research* (1994), edited by Norman Denzin and Yvonna Lincoln.

In the simplest of terms, a paradigm is "a basic set of beliefs that guide action" (Denzin & Lincoln, 2003, p. 245). Paradigms are, however, much more complicated than this simple definition implies. All paradigms that guide field research have four major, interrelated beliefs about **ontology, epistemology, methodology,** and **axiology.**

The ontological questions include *What is the nature of reality? Is there a way that things "really work?" Are there laws that can explain the relationships between things? Is there a "Truth" that can be known? Is there a "reality out there" that good research can discover* (Denzin & Lincoln, 1994)? Questions like these fall under the rubric of ontology. Adherents to different paradigms will answer this set of questions in different ways.

Epistemology refers to the relationship between the knower and the known. The central epistemological question asks, *Is what is learned independent of the researcher?* Those researchers who have one set of epistemological beliefs might say that the social reality "out there" exists independently of the researcher. An alternative view is that there are multiple realities and a relationship exists between the researcher and what can be learned from the research.

Methodology focuses on the procedures for understanding the world. The methodological question is, *How should the researcher go about finding out about social reality?* Methodology involves more than just the techniques used for collecting data, such as interviewing. Rather, methodology encompasses the entire research design, including such questions as whether the research should be qualitative or quantitative and what kind of sampling procedures and logic should be used. One's methodological beliefs help determine whether research is best conducted by controlling the research process, such as through experiments, or by allowing it to develop in a natural setting.

Axiology is concerned with values and ethics. Typical axiological questions are, *What is the role of values in the research process? Should researchers be disinterested scientists or emotionally engaged in the research?*

Particular configurations of answers to ontological, epistemological, methodological, and axiological questions are organized into paradigms. Conceding that there is an amazing amount of confusion about the different paradigms that guide field research, I will simplify this presentation by starting with three frequently used paradigms: positivist, interpretive, and critical.

Positivist Paradigm

A **positivist** paradigm is associated with the dominant model of scientific research. Quantitative researchers almost always use a positivist paradigm, whereas only some field researchers situate their work within it. Although you may not have heard of a "positivist paradigm," I suspect you know what it is. Within this paradigm, the process of scientific discovery begins with a theory. Using deductive logic, the researcher derives a testable hypothesis from the theory. Then data are collected to test the hypothesis. On the basis of the results of the data analysis, the researcher decides whether there is empirical support for the hypothesis. Some researchers believe that this model of science provides the only legitimate methodology for conducting scientific research.

To illustrate this paradigm, let's consider a line or two from a DiFranco song. In "True Story of What Was," DiFranco (2004) sings "real is real regardless of what you try to say, or say away, real is real relentless." Although I am not implying that DiFranco would identify herself as a positivist, the sentiment that the "real is real regardless" is consistent with the underlying *ontological assumption* of positivism that an objective reality exists. For positivists, social reality is stable and patterned so it can be known through rigorous investigation. Post-positivists concede that we might never know reality perfectly, but they argue that the accumulated efforts of our research will move us toward discovering what is real. The overarching goal of this paradigm involves just this search for probabilistic causal laws of social behavior. The hope of this paradigm is that social science research can lead to prediction and even control.

Miles and Huberman (1994), who are well known for their work on how to analyze qualitative data, frame their work within a positivist paradigm. They provide the following excellent summary of their ontological beliefs about social reality:

> That means we think that social phenomena exist not only in the minds but also in the objective world—and that some lawful and reasonably stable relationships are to be found among them. The lawfulness comes from the regularities and sequences that link together phenomena. From these patterns we can derive constructs that underline individual and social life. The fact that most of those constructs are invisible to the human eye does not make them invalid. After all, we all are surrounded by lawful physical mechanisms of which we're, at most, remotely aware.
>
> In other words, social phenomena, such as language, decisions, conflicts, and hierarchies, exist objectively in the world and exert strong influences over human activities because people construe them in common ways. Things that are believed become real and can be inquired into. (p. 4)

The *epistemological position* of positivists is that what can be learned about the social world exists independently of the researcher. Thus, field researchers who operate within this paradigm often do not include reflexive statements in their final products or integrate themselves into the text to the same degree as do researchers in other paradigms.

The *axiological stance* regarding research conducted within this tradition is that it should be objective and value free. For example, although the researcher might actually care deeply about the participants in his or her project or, alternately, find their behaviors highly offensive, according to the positivist tradition the final manuscript should not provide the reader any clue to the researcher's reactions. In other words, the researcher's feelings or values should have no place in the research results. Because of the axiological belief in value neutrality, within the positivist framework the final products of research are written in the voice of the neutral, dispassionate researcher.

Reliability, validity, and **generalizability** are key *methodological concerns* of research framed within a positivist framework. Researchers might use probabilistic sampling, complete observations with specific foci at predetermined times, and hold structured interviews.

Paradigms other than positivism often guide qualitative research. Unfortunately, defining and discussing these other paradigms is no easy task, as researchers have difficulty agreeing on what they are, how many exist, what they should be called, and how they are organized in relationship to each other. For the purposes of this guide, however, I have chosen to follow the convention of referring to two other common paradigms for qualitative researchers as interpretive and critical.

Interpretive Paradigm

Adherents of an **interpretive** paradigm hold a view of the social world different from that of positivists. Their *ontological belief* is that there is no objective social reality but instead multiple realities. A lyric from DiFranco (1995) is consistent with the ontological perspective of multiple realities: "what might be justice to you, might not be justice to me." That is, the social world is not an entity in and of itself but is local, temporally and historically situated, fluid, context-specific, and shaped in conjunction with the researcher (Guba & Lincoln, 1994, p.109).

Research undertaken with an interpretive paradigm in mind focuses on social relationships, as well as the mechanisms and processes through which members in a setting navigate and create their social worlds. Thus, the researcher using an interpretive paradigm asks what kinds of things people do, how they do them, what purposes activities serve, and what they mean to the participants. In other words, the researcher becomes interested in the meanings, symbols, beliefs, ideas, and feelings given or attached to objects, events, activities, and others by participants in the setting. The goals of field research for scholars who use an interpretive paradigm involve empathetic understanding of participants' day-to-day experiences and an increased awareness of the multiple meanings given to the routine and problematic events by those in the setting.

Although the notion of a stable social reality is inconsistent with an interpretive paradigm, few deny there is a physical reality. For example, it is doubtful that a field researcher would claim that a wall is a social rather than a physical construct, and then, to support the claim, would attempt to walk through it. However, what is important to field researchers is the socially significant meanings attached to the physical world. Think of an American flag, for instance. Is such a flag merely pieces of multi-colored material sewn together in a consistent pattern—or is it a complex web of socially reflective emotions, symbolism, and ideals? If it is merely the former, then why do some people argue for a constitutional amendment that would prohibit burning it? In order to fully grasp the implications of the setting and the individuals who inhabit it, the field researcher seeks to understand not the nature of the physical entity but that of the meanings the participants attach to it.

As a result of the *epistemological belief* that what is learned in research does not exist independently of the researcher, this paradigm does not emphasize objectivity. This lack of emphasis on objectivity does not mean, however, that the researcher can use the interpretive paradigm as an excuse for injecting personal bias into the project or for manipu-lating the evidence to demonstrate a point he or she wants to make. Rather, adherents of an interpretive paradigm believe that what researchers learn from the participants depends, in part, on their own status charac-teristics, values, and behaviors. And taking this into account during all phases of the research can increase the validity, or **trustworthiness**, of the research.

The *methodology* of an interpretive paradigm often includes inter-actions with and observations of participants in the setting. As DiFranco suggests, "you got to look outside your eyes, you got to think outside your brain, you got to walk outside your life, to where the neighborhood changes" (DiFranco, 1993). Understanding how people live and inter-pret their lives requires that researchers move, often literally, out of their own worlds and into the setting of the participants. At the same time, adherents of an interpretive paradigm believe that they cannot totally leave behind their understanding of the world. Thus, they have no pretense of objectivity, and their *axiological stance* rejects the view that value neutrality is essential to the research process. Consequently, reflec-tions are included in the final manuscript about the ways that their val-ues and other characteristics might influence what was learned. The final manuscript is often written as a first-person account of the researcher's immersion in the setting.

Although I have referred to the paradigm just discussed as interpre-tive, not everyone would have used this name in describing or defining it. For example, some scholars consider an interpretive paradigm equivalent to or only slightly different from constructivism. Others include constructivism as a subset of an interpretive paradigm. Again, it bears noting that whereas the positivist paradigm is easy enough to explain, other paradigms are more difficult because scholars disagree about what they are, what to call them, and how to define them.

Critical Paradigm

Another paradigm often used by qualitative researchers is a **critical** paradigm, which often seeks to empower the people in a setting and to work toward meaningful social change (Neuman, 1991, p. 81). Field researchers who are guided by a critical paradigm might want to document, understand, and change the way that powerful groups oppress powerless groups. Once again I turn to DiFranco as a means of exploring this paradigm. In "From Trickle Down" (1999) she sings, "and they explained about the cutbacks all with earnest frowns, but what they didn't say was the plant was slowly shutting down, and they're building condos down river from where the plant had been." DiFranco's lines exemplify the sorts of situations that spark researchers who use a critical paradigm to guide their work. If she happened to be a researcher guided by a critical paradigm, DiFranco might be expressing her desire to understand how the community is affected by the factory closing and to suggest the means by which the unemployed workers could be empowered to respond to negative effects.

During her hypothetical field research, DiFranco might focus her attention on social institutions, such as the schools and health care. For example, she would want to know what changes occurred in the school system as a result of the eroding property tax base. Did the schools have to discontinue music and after-school sports programs, like soccer? Did the district's most dedicated and experienced teachers move to other locations where they could earn more money? Did the school's physical plant fall into disrepair because needed repairs could not be made?

A critical paradigm is consistent with the interpretive *ontological position* that there is no single "reality out there." Additionally, researchers who work within this paradigm stress that social reality is shaped by historical, social, political, cultural, and economic factors, as well as by ethnic, racial, and gendered structures, among others.

Epistemologically, scholars who use a critical paradigm believe that the researcher is not independent from what is researched and that the findings of research are mediated through his or her values.

Within the critical paradigm, the *axiological belief* is that values are important to the research and should be clearly articulated in the work and to the participants. An important value that often accompanies this type of research is a desire to eradicate social injustices. Whereas positivist researchers adhere to principles of objectivity, those anchored in the critical tradition might write passionately about the lives of the participants.

Methodologically, the scholar who follows a critical paradigm often takes a macro approach to research. That is, he or she includes factors from the setting beyond the individuals in it—such as oppressive policies, laws, and funding allocations. Analysis that springs from a critical paradigm often includes emphasis on the negative effects of racism or unequal gender relations. As a result, variants or subsets of this paradigm exist that focus specifically on studying a setting and its participants from a particular critical stance, such as feminism and Marxism. The critical researcher frequently includes analysis of historical, social, and cultural events that extend beyond the setting. Documenting, and at times reducing, the negative implications of capitalism, imperialism, and unequal power relationships lies at the heart of much work undertaken within the critical paradigm.

Understanding paradigms can be a difficult task for the beginning researcher, yet an awareness of them is vital because their underlying assumptions affect most aspects of research. Different sets of assumptions lead to different standards for how the research is conducted and how the results are presented and evaluated. Additionally, the types of relationships formed between the researcher and the participants of a study depend, in part, upon the paradigm guiding the research. Fortunately, the process of learning field research is rendered easier because the different paradigms share much of the same methodology. However, the methodological differences among the paradigms have such huge implications that their study as a whole cannot be ignored.

Given the controversies and confusion inherent in paradigms, graduate students should be particularly careful when selecting their committee to ensure that all of its members are comfortable with the paradigmatic underpinning of the research. I have attended far too many dissertation proposal defenses that progressed with difficulty because a committee member continued to insist on the need for testable hypotheses for research not framed by a positivist paradigm. Fortunately, if you are an undergraduate who is required to complete a field research project, your instructor most likely will provide you with guidance as to which paradigm is most appropriate for your research.

Because an interpretive paradigm is arguably the most common paradigm used by field researchers, this book is largely framed within this paradigm. Nonetheless, I again remind you that it is not the only one adopted or espoused by field researchers. I conclude this section with the observation that the chapter "Paradigmatic Controversies, Contradictions, and Emerging Confluences," written by Lincoln and Guba (2003) and found in the second edition of *The Landscape of Qualitative Research: Theories and Issues* (Denzin & Lincoln, 2003), is aptly named—and a must-read for the student who seeks a more complete understanding of the difficulties inherent in the study of paradigms.

Theory

In addition to deciding which paradigm to adopt, researchers must also make decisions about theory, the second component of field research. Complicated and sometimes heated discussions also exist about the relationship between theory and field research (see, for examples, Hammersley, 1992, and Wacquant, 2002). Because of space limitations, here I will address only two closely related questions in the debate about the relationship between theory and field research: (1) What role does theory play in field research? and (2) What counts as theory?

Role of Theory

The first issue involves the role of theory in field research. I once heard a sociologist say, "Qualitative research without theory is just words." I no longer recall who said it or if it was meant literally, but it nicely captures the view that theory is essential to all types of field research. From this perspective, theory provides the guiding structure for data collection and analysis. Without theory, researchers would have to scoop up everything during data collection and dump it all out in the final manuscript, a process that would result in nothing more than a literal "data dump," impressive in volume but ultimately meaningless in terms of research value. In fact, Wolcott (1994) compares this technique to that of a student who writes everything he or she knows on an essay exam when the answer to the question is not forthcoming. A final manuscript not guided by theory, like the essay exam, might include lots of information but still not be very good. Wacquant (2002) gives this advice for improving the final manuscript: "far from being antithetical, vivid ethnography and powerful theory are complementary and . . . the best strategy to strengthen the former is to bolster the latter" (p. 1524).

A contrasting view is that theory is not always needed. Evaluation research, for example, could be conducted without the guiding hand of theory, and research that consists primarily of thick descriptions might be atheoretical as well. Others (see, for example, Wolcott, 1994) challenge the view that descriptions can be atheoretical. Likewise, Wacquant (2002), whose writing at times is not for the fainthearted, asserts that there is "no such thing as a description, thick or thin, that does not engage a theory, understood as a principle of pertinence and protomodel of the phenomenon at hand adumbrating its nature, constituents, and articulation" (p. 1524).

Although Wacquant's "definition" of what he means by theory is wonderfully dense, it does foreshadow another issue in the debate about the relationship between theory and field research.

What Is Theory?

This second issue involves what counts as theory. Are theories a set of interlinked propositions that explain some social phenomenon? Are they ideas we have about how the world works and why people do what they do? Do orienting frameworks, conceptual lenses, sensitizing concepts, causal models, disciplinary perspectives, philosophical perspectives, worldviews, and distinct social science theories all count as theory? Can a theory and a paradigm be the same thing? Is using theoretical concepts, such as power and social capital, derived from a variety of theories, sufficient for claims that one's analysis is theoretically informed?

My single answer to all of these questions is a simple "yes." Since all of these definitions and concepts can influence how we understand the world and our research, I believe that for the purposes of field research all of them can potentially count as theory. For me, what varies is the degree to which our theories are discipline-specific, explicit, shared, and sophisticated.

Well before we became social scientists, we developed concepts and theories about how the social world works. We have theories about our neighbors' behavior, national politics, buying and selling things, raising children, and so on. In short, we already have theory embedded in our worldviews. As social scientists, however, we realize that theories that guide our research transcend mere common-sense understanding of the world. Indeed, with a developing sociological imagination and awareness of different theoretical perspectives, an exciting moment for students occurs when they first discover that sociology "isn't common sense." Of course, the level of theoretical insight that informs our research varies from researcher to researcher. For example, undergraduates might start a field research project with sensitizing concepts, such as gender relations, because they have noticed that gender matters in social interactions. In contrast, a Ph.D. student might frame his or her work within a well-developed theoretical tradition. Yet, the key point is that the undergraduate and graduate student alike share some measure of theoretical insight, no matter how varied in degree. What is important is to *explicitly* state one's theoretical frame, regardless of what it is called or the level of its complexity.

With notable exceptions, I do not believe that researchers can conduct their research without some kind of theory, regardless of what it formally might be called. Theories are important for selecting a topic, creating goals, developing research questions, and collecting, analyzing, and interpreting data.

This was the case for Chenault (2004), who, prior to starting her dissertation, theoretically identified herself as a critical race theorist. One of the tenets of critical race theory is that in many cases laws and policies increase rather than eradicate inequality. When it became clear to Chenault that she was interested in studying a resident council in public housing communities, she quickly became curious not just about whether a disjunction existed between the actual activities of the resident council and what the Department of Housing and Urban Development (HUD) expected it to do, but also about what might account for any differences that she might discover. Thus, in keeping with the tenets of her chosen theory, Chenault began data collection with a content analysis of HUD policies relevant to the resident council. She also used critical race theory during her analysis. Yet, when she found that this theory alone was insufficient for explaining some of what she found, she called upon other theories and theoretical concepts. Like many field researchers, she was influenced by her theoretical perspective throughout her work, but she was not blinded by it during data collection nor wedded to it during the analysis.

As you develop your theoretical framework, you can turn your attention to the tradition of inquiry that is appropriate for answering your research questions.

Traditions of Inquiry

The third element of field research involves selecting the appropriate tradition of inquiry, often called a strategy of inquiry, a research tradition, or type of research. (Throughout this guide, I use these terms interchangeably). The researcher's chosen paradigm and theoretical approach do not usually dictate which tradition of inquiry is adopted, although the paradigm certainly influences how the research within a particular tradition is conducted. Instead, the researcher chooses the strategy of inquiry independently, selecting the most appropriate one for answering the project's research questions.

Qualitative researchers use many different strategies of inquiry: case studies, biographies, **grounded theory**, clinical research, phenomenological research, evaluation research, participatory action research, ethnographies, and scholar activist approaches (Kershaw, 2005). Most strategies can be broken down into subtypes. For example, different types of evaluation research include responsive evaluation (Stake, 2004) and utilization-focused evaluation (Patton, 1997).

This guide focuses on a single strategy of inquiry: field research. Field research itself has different names and types. For example, "participant observation" and "ethnography" are two common names for field research. Different types of **ethnographies** include **ethnographic case study**, **critical ethnography**, and the more controversial **autoethnography** (Morse & Richards, 2002). Although this guide will be most useful to those who choose ethnography as their strategy of inquiry, much of this book is relevant to any strategy that includes fieldwork or uses qualitative data.

Once researchers have decided upon the paradigm that will guide their research, articulated their theory, and selected field research as their strategy of inquiry, they are ready to move to designing the methodological structure of their work. Features of methodology are presented in the following chapter.

Chapter Highlights

1. Paradigms are sets of beliefs that guide almost every aspect of field research.

2. Paradigms consist of ontological, epistemological, axiological, and methodological assumptions.

3. Methodology is the overarching procedures used during field research.

4. Positivist, interpretive, and critical are three paradigms frequently used by field researchers.

5. Theories are implicitly or explicitly embedded in all field research.

6. Field research is one of many strategies of inquiry used by qualitative researchers.

Exercises

---

1. Review the ontological, epistemological, axiological, and methodological assumptions of positivist, interpretive, and critical paradigms. Which of these is most consistent with your beliefs? Explain why.

2. Is it possible to include values in the research process and still conduct unbiased research? Justify your answer.

3. Select a theory of your choice. Describe a field research project that could be informed by this theory.

4. Find two journal articles that used ethnography as the research strategy. Summarize the role of theory in each article. What paradigm was used to guide the work? If it is not explicitly stated, which one do you think best applies? Justify your answer.

5

Methodology

The fourth component of field research is *methodology*, a term that refers to the larger research design that one follows when engaging in research, rather than just the specific methods used for collecting data. Methodology includes such things as sampling, gaining entrée, resolving ethical concerns, and maintaining relationships in the field. The techniques used to collect the data, such as interviews and observations, fall under what I refer to as methods and are covered in later chapters.

Sampling

Let's pretend that you are interested in studying high school science classes. You have access to four high schools, each with eight science classes. Even if you love science, observing all 32 classes is probably more than you want to undertake. You decide to conduct long-term observations in one class, but which class? How will you decide? To answer questions such as these, field researchers use sampling procedures.

Two major types of sampling are probability sampling and purposeful sampling. You might be familiar with probability sampling, which includes such types as random, systematic, and stratified sampling. These sampling methods are used to select a sample from a larger population in such a way that the sample is representative of the population from which it was drawn. A primary purpose of using probability sampling is to be able to statistically generalize the results from the sample to the population. Probability sampling is usually used when a large sample is desired.

Although probability sampling is primarily associated with quantitative work, field researchers can use probability sampling. A field researcher might, for example, systematically select every fifth person who enters a jewelry store and interview him or her. Fieldwork conducted by a large team of researchers might use probability sampling.

For the most part, field researchers use purposeful sampling or theoretical sampling. The number of cases selected with purposeful sampling is often small: One person, such as a high school principal, might be chosen for an in-depth examination of his daily routine; two locations might be compared, such as health clubs that serve different types of clients; or 22 workers in a meat packing plant might be observed and interviewed (Wolcott, 1994).

The key to purposeful sampling is to select cases for systematic study that are information rich (Patton, 1990). As with probability sampling, there are different types of purposeful sampling. From the array of available options, field researchers select the strategy that meets the purpose and goals of their research. I find Patton's explanations of different types of purposeful sampling particularly informative, so I have modified one of his summary tables and present it in Figure 5.1. The types of sampling he describes can be used for sampling settings or groups, individuals, observation times, documents, other artifacts, and so on.

There is a misconception that field researchers rely on convenience sampling. To the contrary, convenience sampling is the weakest form of sampling and is avoided when possible.

Determining the size of the sample for field research is closer to *Goldilocks and the Three Bears* than it is to a mathematical formula. The sample should not be too small or too large. It should be "just right." Too small of a sample can lead to misleading results. Samples that are too large make in-depth analysis of each case impossible. Someplace in between too small and too large is "just right."

Obviously, this still leaves us with the question, how big should the sample be? This question has no easy answer. When selecting individuals to be interviewed, a good starting point is 20. Then, continue to interview until you have at least five new cases that fail to add anything new to the analysis.

Do not hold too firmly to the notion of 20 as being "just right." In truth, how many cases you select depends upon a host of factors—the purpose of the research, the research questions, the number of participants available, and the time and resources of the researcher (Patton, 1990). The appropriate sample size also is affected by what is being sampled—research sites, times for observing, documents to analyze, and so on.

Extreme or deviant case	Selecting cases that have unusual manifestations of the phenomenon of interest
Intensity	Selecting information-rich cases that manifest the phenomenon intensely, but not extremely
Maximum variation	Selecting cases that are considerably different on the dimensions of interest
Homogeneous	Selecting cases that are similar to each other
Typical case	Selecting cases that are typical, normal, average
Stratified	Selecting cases from different subgroups
Critical case	Selecting cases that have potential for logical generalizations and maximum application of information to other cases
Snowball or chain	Selecting cases from referrals by participants
Criterion	Selecting cases based on them meeting some criterion of interest
Theory-based	Selecting cases that manifest theoretical constructs of interest
Confirming and disconfirming	Selecting cases that have potential for supporting or refuting initial analysis
Opportunistic	Selecting cases that are unexpectedly available
Random	Selecting a relatively small number of cases using a probability sampling procedure
Political	Selecting or avoiding politically sensitive cases
Convenience	Selecting cases that require little effort or forethought
Combination	Selecting cases by mixing purposeful sampling with probability sampling

Figure 5.1   Purposeful Sampling Strategies

SOURCE: From *Qualitative Evaluation and Research Methods*, Second Edition (pp. 182–183), by M. Q. Patton, 1990, Newbury Park, CA: Sage. Copyright 1994 by Sage Publications, Inc. Reprinted with permission.

Gaining Entrée

Remember our friend Herbie Goldfarb from *The Milagro Beanfield War* (Nichols, 1974)? Herbie was excited about being in Milagro, so he assumed the members of the community would be as eager to have him there as he was to be there. As often occurs in field research, however, this was a false assumption. Herbie might have been more successful in Milagro had he known some of the procedures that successful field researchers use to gain entrée to a setting.

Gaining entrée is a complicated process, and the particular route one takes to gain entrée affects the rest of the research. For example, procedures for gaining access depend on the location of your setting and whether you are conducting the research alone or as a member of a team (Burgess, 1991).

As noted previously, not all settings are open to everyone; some require that you gain permission before entering. The individuals who play a key role in granting or denying access are referred to in field research literature as gatekeepers. In addition to controlling access, gatekeepers control the flow of interactions within a setting (Burgess, 1991). By thus limiting when the researcher gets to come and go, who he or she talks to and for how long, and what can be observed, they effectively dictate what kinds of data and information are available (Burgess, 1991). Consequently, the gatekeeper can wield a great deal of power over a study's outcomes. Throughout the research process, gaining access is usually negotiated and renegotiated (Burgess, 1991). Johnson aptly describes the process of gaining entrée as a continuing, "progressive series of negotiations rather than a one-shot agreement" (1975, p. 176).

To facilitate gaining entrée, explain who you are and why you are conducting the research. The gatekeeper might need to know who will see your field notes, listen to the tapes from the interviews, and read the final manuscript. Make sure that you talk about issues of informed consent, confidentiality, and the use of pseudonyms. For those of you who will undertake field research for a class project, a letter of introduction from your instructor written on official letterhead might help you in some settings.

That said, although gatekeepers require a reasonable explanation of your research focus, they need not know everything about it. Sometimes simply sharing your research questions sufficiently reassures the gatekeeper. In any case, if this individual does not have a good sense of what you are doing, your chances of being denied access increase greatly. Be prepared to explain how your goals of wanting to understand the day-to-day interactions in a setting are different from wanting to evaluate or judge the setting. Remember that similar information must be provided to both the formal and informal gatekeepers and be aware that each person in your chosen setting is "to a greater or lesser degree a gatekeeper" (Burgess, 1991, p. 48).

Although I provide the above practical advice, access to a setting is sometimes gained simply by a large amount of creativity, luck, and a willingness to seize the moment. A string of events led Duneier (1999) to an opportunity for gaining access to sidewalk magazine vendors in Greenwich Village. Hakim Hasam, a central figure in an earlier book by Duneier, introduced Marvin Martin to him. Duneier explained how through Marvin he gained access to the world of the vendors:

> As he thought about going back to New York, he lamented that his business partner, Ron, was going through a stage of being unreliable. Every time Marvin left the table to place bets at Off-Track Betting, he had to depend on Ron to remain by the table; if Ron was drunk or high, he might abandon the table, and it would be taken by the police.
>
> A thought occurred to me. I could work for Marvin during the coming summer. I would learn a lot more about the sidewalk, if I worked as a vendor myself, than I would by merely observing or doing interviews, and he would have his table covered. So I proposed that I work at this table for three months and give him the money I made. "What will the fellas think when I have a white guy working for me all summer?" he asked. We decided he should just tell them the truth— I was there to do research on a book about the block—and he said he would think about it. (p. 334)

Although it took some time for Duneier to be sufficiently accepted by the other vendors, he at least had a place to be, something to do, and permission to be on the scene from one of the informal gatekeepers on the street.

Numerous other factors can affect the researcher's chances of gaining access to a setting. For example, gender plays a crucial role. Field researchers of the "wrong" gender sometimes are denied access. For example, women may find it more difficult to get permission to study settings that are generally dominated by men, such as professional sports teams. Alternatively, a group dominated by a particular gender may view a researcher of the other gender as a delightful addition to the setting, making it easier for permission to be gained.

Just as your gender can work for or against you in complicated ways as you attempt to enter your research setting, so too can your chances be affected by your race, ethnicity, age, sexual orientation, social class, or other personal characteristics. As noted above, Marvin, who helped Duneier (1999) get access to the street vendors, worried that the researcher's race might present a problem. Remember, too, that people often react to the intersection of these characteristics. Not only was Duneier White in a setting predominated by Black men, but also his clothing, speech, and diction were different. Should he have attempted to alter these last three characteristics to fit in? The answer in this case and others is "no." Attempts to more than minimally change one's clothing, speech, or diction are often ineffectual—and potentially insulting.

Arrival in the Field

Upon their arrival in the field, researchers can find themselves in unexpected situations. When I think about some of the situations that have occurred, I am reminded of the line from one of Hunter S. Thompson's books: "Bad craziness, but it never got weird enough for me" (1979). Some of these situations would, in fact, have been "too weird" for me, and I would probably have retreated hastily. However, many field researchers have persevered despite early days of "bad craziness." Indeed, Wax suggests that smooth early interactions in a setting are not only rare, but also suspect (1971, p. 17). Wax certainly knows from firsthand experience how difficult one's arrival in a setting can be. For the first six weeks she was on-site at a Japanese American relocation camp, she felt as though she were losing her mind because no one would talk to her. During the early days of their research, other researchers have described feeling "stupid, clumsy, and less than human" and "full of disorientation, shock, and disequilibrium" (p. 19).

Sometimes the best way to approach one's early days in a setting is with a good sense of humor. When I am in an extremely uncomfortable situation, for example, I try to reassure myself that the experience will someday make an entertaining story at a party. Wax (1971) provides similar advice: "Painful and humiliating experiences are easier to talk about if one does not take them too seriously, and it is less distressing to picture oneself as a clown or figure of fun than as a dolt or a neurotic" (p. 19).

Regardless of how the researcher handles the situation, feeling out of place or even worse is to be expected when one first begins the fieldwork portion of a project. Such feelings are in fact quite common: The very role of field research in unfamiliar settings requires that you take yourself out of your own comfortable world and enter one that is new to you.

The purpose of this section is not to scare you away from field research but to help you appreciate the difficulties of arriving in a setting so that you can be prepared to deal with the potential stresses such an endeavor might bring. Also, I would mislead you if I pretended that early interactions in a setting are simply experiences to get through so that you can proceed with the business of doing "real" research. In fact, the initial period of immersion in the setting lays the groundwork for the rest of a field research project. Everything that follows is affected by these early interactions, particularly as they hold the potential for introducing to you the actors who will play key roles in your project.

Key Actors

One factor that can help the field researcher move beyond the awkward, and often scary, early days of field research is the assistance of one or more members in the setting. If you can establish **rapport** and procure the cooperation of at least one member of the setting, you have a better chance of proceeding with the types of interactions and observations necessary for a successful project.

Field researchers sometimes refer to the person who rescues and assists them as a **key actor** or key insider, a member of the setting who is willing to act as a guide and assistant. Historically, this person has been called an informant, but many of us prefer to move away from this term because of its negative connotations.

A key actor might be someone the researcher knows prior to undertaking the research or one of the formal or informal gatekeepers with whom a relationship has been developed during the gaining entrée stages of the project. Usually, the key insider is someone the researcher met in the early days of the research who, for often-unknown reasons, is willing to "adopt" the researcher and become her or his mentor and guide.

Interactions with others in the setting are often easier to establish if the key actor makes introductions. This person can help the researcher gain entrée, establish rapport, provide explanations, and perform a host of other useful tasks. The key actor might also tell the researcher when he or she has committed a social faux pas or is in potential danger (Wax, 1971). The key insider helps resocialize the field researcher to the ways of the members in the setting.

Although key actors provide a valuable service, costs also are involved with relying on insiders as your guides. One drawback is that key actors have their own perspectives, biographies, and agendas that influence what they see, think, and feel. Although important, the perspectives of the insider may run counter to those of most members of the setting. Consequently, the insider's understanding of the setting should be considered only one of many perspectives and not taken as representative of the group as a whole.

Another disadvantage of working with an insider is that by doing so the researcher runs the risk of isolating himself or herself from some members of the setting. For example, Hakim Hasam, an important key actor in Duneier's (1999) work on street vendors, was well respected by other vendors except Muhammad. Thus, although Hasam was an extremely valuable resource, Duneier had to be "less than sincere" from time to time about his relationship to Hasam if he wanted to have access to all the vendors (p. 336). As a result, Duneier struggled with the recognition that his presentation of self led him into that gray area where fieldwork at times becomes a "morally ambiguous enterprise" (p. 336). The situation for Duneier would have been considerably worse if he had discovered that Hasam was not well liked.

If the researcher learns too late that the key actor with whom he or she has connected actually impeded, rather than helped, the research, ethical issues present an even greater concern. Most of us know the pain of trying to disentangle ourselves from a friendship that is no longer desired. Because of the risks, as well as the benefits, of the participation of key actors, researchers are usually cautious about letting these individuals have too much input into the parameters of the study. At the same time, fieldwork is often a cooperative venture undertaken with participants in a setting, rather than a hierarchical activity with the researcher wielding all power. Thus, as a **member** of the setting, the key actor possesses a perspective that is as important as but not superior to any other. Through careful and continual study of field notes and persistent reflection on the research process as it unfolds, the researcher can keep tabs on whether he or she is unwittingly permitting the key actor to unduly influence the direction of the project.

In addition to gaining entrée, entering a new environment, and finding a key actor, ethical concerns are ever present.

Informed Consent

Chapter 2 of this guide discussed the issue of Institutional Review Board approval, a step that is required for any study focusing on human subjects.

In order to gain such approval, the researcher must have a plan for getting informed consent that the board considers ethical. Sometimes gaining permission from gatekeepers and obtaining informed consent from participants in the setting is the same thing. After all, both formal and informal gatekeepers also can be members in the setting.

Liebow's (1994) research provides a good example of gaining entrée and obtaining informed consent simultaneously from informal gatekeepers. After he retired on disability from 20 years on the job as an anthropologist with the National Institute of Mental Health, Liebow volunteered at a soup kitchen and shelter. Because he thoroughly enjoyed the interactions with the women at the shelter, he decided to undertake a research project. He first obtained permission from the formal gatekeeper, the shelter director. Because Liebow was already known to the shelter director as a competent and respected volunteer, he was able to obtain permission simply by requesting it. However, this was only one level of gatekeeping that he needed to address. He knew that access also was controlled by informal gatekeepers, specifically key shelter residents. He had to obtain permission from these individuals, as well as the rest of the setting's members. Gaining permission from these women was a fairly easy task, but one with strings attached. In the preface of his book, Liebow recounts his experience:

> "Listen," I said at the dinner table one evening, after getting permission to do a study from the shelter director. "I want your permission to take notes. I want to go home at night and write down what I can remember about the things you say and do. Maybe I'll write a book about homeless women." Most of the dozen or so women there nodded their heads or simply shrugged. All except Regina. Her acceptance was conditional. "Only if you promise not to publish before I do," she said. Believing that neither one of us, for different reasons, would ever publish anything in the future, I readily agreed. (p. ix)

For the researcher, this informal agreement over dinner permitted the study to continue, but it carried a prohibition of sorts: It essentially established the rules or ethical guidelines by which Liebow could publish his results. Fortunately, Liebow eventually received Regina's permission to publish; otherwise, according to the ethical standards established in the field, he would have been bound by their earlier agreement.

Conducting research in which all members participate voluntarily through informed consent is easier to accomplish in theory than in practice. First, informed consent is not static: Once permission is given it can be withdrawn at any time, and the ethical researcher has no choice but to honor the request of a member who no longer wishes to participate. Liebow's (1994) work provides an example of this. Some women agreed to participate in his research project, but then withdrew their permission, one at an extremely late date in the process. He writes,

> Originally, I had asked three homeless women and the director of a shelter to write comments on the manuscript. One of the women, after reading a draft of the manuscript, and for reasons not clear to me, angrily decided she did not want to be in the book at all. She did agree to allow herself to be quoted (but not described) in a couple of places. All other references to her were deleted at her request. Similarly, in the second year one of the more distinctive and more troubled women told me she wanted nothing to do with me or anything I might write. . . . We had gotten along well until the day she saw me in earnest conversation with a woman who had become her enemy. On the theory that "the friend of my enemy is my enemy," she refused to talk to me thereafter (as she had refused to talk to some of the women as well). Also, from that day on, to her I was no longer "Elliot" but "Idiot," as in "Here comes Idiot again to seduce all the women." (p. xvii)

Another difficulty inherent in informed consent is that the researcher might find it impossible to inform everyone who enters a setting that a study is in progress. Van Maanen's (1982) work capably illustrates the difficulties and implications of not informing everyone in a setting. Whereas all of the officers in Van Maanen's study of the police were informed of his role as observer, their agreement to participate fully in the project was granted only after they felt he had passed several tests—not all of which were legal—demonstrating his loyalty and trustworthiness. However, Van Maanen did not extend informed consent to the citizens he encountered. Since he dressed as a plainclothes police officer, most citizens assumed he was a member of the police force, yet "at no time was a citizen ever let in on the partial charade" (p. 113).

Partly because of his agreements with the police officers, Van Maanen decided not to inform the citizens he encountered while "on the job." In defense of this decision, he argued that once he obtained police consent to act as a participant observer, then he had an obligation to participate. Thus, Van Maanen had to back up or assist police officers acting in the line of duty. He writes,

> It is also worth noting that the height of moral duplicity would be to create this sort of partnership impression among the people one studies

and then refuse to act in line with the implicit bargain such an impression conveys. For me to pose as a friend of the police and then not back them up on a potentially risky adventure, an adventure they may well have undertaken only because of the additional safety they believed my presence provided, would be to violate the very premises of ethnographic research and the importance human relationships play in its enactment. (p. 114)

As researchers we end up on shaky ground when we start making decisions about when informed consent is important. At the same time, the dynamics of field research are such that the researcher often has to make this decision many times during field research. Some Institutional Review Boards require you to explain your informed consent procedures for both the regular participants in the setting and those who might not be but enter it nonetheless.

Field Relationships

Unless we live in total isolation, much of our everyday lives are deeply affected by our relationships. If I asked you to talk about your college experiences, for example, no doubt you would spend a lot of time discussing your relationships with others. Your relationships are probably the most wonderful and sometimes the most painful components of your college life. Daily you engage in relationships of varying degrees and types. You might have a close romantic relationship with a significant other. Probably you have some formal and fairly distant relationships with some of the university's faculty and staff. You have informal, positive relationships with other students. Sometimes your relationships might be negative, as with an ex-roommate. You might have relationships that serve an explicit function, such as when you work with others on a class project. No doubt the dynamics of your many relationships occasionally change and greatly affect how you perceive the quality of your day-to-day life.

Just as your relationships are deeply embedded in your college experiences, relationships similarly affect the field research process. Participating in relationships with members of the setting provides the basis for the interpretive process considered so central to field research. These relationships supply the foundation for what field researchers come to know in the setting. Formation of relationships begins as early as the moment you try to gain entrée to a setting.

A song by the artist Ferron contains the line "Life don't go clickity-clack along a straight-lined track, it comes together, and it comes apart" (1980). This description captures the unexpected and decidedly nonlinear nature of field research, including the relationships the researcher establishes with the participants. The life of the field researcher and the lives of those in the setting under study repeatedly come together and come apart—not fully merging, yet never fully independent.

Field research hinges on personal relationships, preferably ones that are egalitarian and not hierarchical. In her field study of the daily lives of two families, Judith Stacey illustrates this precept:

> Choosing my next major research project, I was eager for a "hands-on" engagement in the field. Unschooled in fieldwork research as I was, I did not anticipate the depth or the complexity of the emotional experiences I was about to undergo. My heart, much more than my hands, has been engaged with the people portrayed in this book who so generously agreed to subject their families to my impertinent sociological scrutiny. (1991, p. ix)

Those who have written about field research almost always have acknowledged the importance of field relationships. Even the earliest textbooks on the subject usually include a section on developing rapport with those in the field. The writers of these early texts told us that if we can get along with the participants in the setting and establish trust, they would invariably open up and provide us with a wealth of information that we might not have gotten without the initial establishing of this rapport. Although it is most assuredly more complex than this early view, current advice to field researchers still emphasizes the central need to establish relationships with those in the setting.

As noted in earlier chapters, the issue of trust in field research is not unidirectional. The field researcher strives for trusting relationships that are reciprocal. Therefore, the onus is placed on the researcher to be worthy of the trust, respect, and goodwill of those encountered in the setting. When he undertook his study of homeless women, for example, Liebow (1994) was keenly aware of the importance of reciprocity. He writes,

> It is difficult to exaggerate the importance of this kind of familiarity. It is essential, I believe, in this kind of study—a participation observer kind of study—that relationships be as symmetrical as possible, that there be a quid pro quo; the women needed to know as much about me as I knew about them. (p. xii)

Several of the women even got to know his daughters.

Liebow further illustrates how many field researchers now conceptualize members in a setting as collaborators, not merely subjects to be conned into cooperating. He continues,

> I think of Betty and Louise and many of the other women as friends. As a friend, I owe them friendship. Perhaps I also owe them something because I have so much and they have so little, but I do not feel under any special obligation to them as research subjects. Indeed, I do not think of them as "research subjects." Since they knew what I was trying to do and allowed me to do it, they could just as well be considered collaborators in what might fairly be seen as a cooperative enterprise. (1994, p. xvi)

Once again I turn to the example provided by Duneier's (1999) study of street vendors. His relationships became so strong with these men and women that after the study ended he co-taught a seminar at the University of California, Santa Barbara with Hakim Hasam, assisted by Alice Morin and Marvin Martin, all of whom were vendors.

Developing such rapport is an important first step toward laying the foundation for a productive and satisfying working relationship. It would be nice if at this point I provided you with a neat list of things you could follow to help you achieve rapport with the participants in the setting. Alas, this is not possible. What works in one setting might backfire in another; what works for one of you will not work for others in your class.

Why is it so difficult to provide instructions for developing rapport? Developing rapport requires the same skills you use for making friends, but when we seek new friends we often gravitate toward those who are a bit like us—perhaps they share our interests in music or film, or they are from the same geographical region. Building rapport with potential participants in the field is more complex because they may be considerably different from you; they may be suspicious of your presence; they may be unpleasant to the point of being disgusting; they may use verbal and nonverbal language different than yours; they may be incredibly brilliant, beautiful, talented, and well known; and they may range from boring to fascinating. Your particular configuration of personality styles also will influence your efforts to engage with the potential participants in your research. Further, the status characteristics of all individuals involved affect relationships and rapport in the field—often in very unpredictable ways. Consequently, it is difficult to give specific directions for building rapport.

Honesty, openness, friendliness, and a willingness to get along are usually the best qualities to exhibit when you first undertake contact with participants in the field, and with time most people will respond positively to genuine concern and interest in them (Neuman, 1991, p. 349). However, remember that building rapport is a process that requires constant attention. Neuman warns us that "rapport is easier to lose once it has been built up than to gain in the first place" (p. 349).

Other features of one's biography also will affect the research process. One's physical attractiveness, neatness habits, standards of time, communication skills, physical health, table manners, hair color and style, level of expertise, musical taste, and abilities are just a few of the many potential factors that affect field relationships in complex and often unknown ways. For example, Liebow (1994) shares with his readers some of the personal characteristics he thinks might have shaped his interactions with the homeless women he studied. He writes,

> It is difficult to be precise about how I was perceived by the women. I am 6'1" and weigh about 175 pounds. I had a lot of white hair but was otherwise nondescript. I dressed casually, often in corduroy pants, shirt, and cardigan. The fact that I was Jewish did not seem to matter much one way or another so far as I could tell. . . . Most of the women probably liked having me around. Male companionship was generally in short supply and the women often made a fuss about the few male volunteers. . . . The fact that I had written a book that was available at the library (three or four women took the trouble to read it) enhanced my legitimacy in their eyes. (p. x)

Although the goal of field research is to understand the everyday lives of those in a setting, this understanding is a negotiated process, affected by the interactions between the researcher and the members. The status characteristics and other personal characteristics of all involved influence the nature of the interactions. The inevitable personal and emotional reactions between the researcher and the members in the setting shape the character of the transactions and their interpretations (Emerson, 1988, p. 176).

In addition to topics discussed thus far—sampling, gaining entrée, resolving ethical concerns, arriving in the field, and nurturing field relationships—researchers have to decide whether their methodology will include triangulation, the topic to which I now turn.

Triangulation

Triangulation comes in many colors and is central to ensuring the quality of field research. Using multiple methods for data collection is a form of triangulation, as is the involvement of multiple researchers. Data from multiple sources of information can be triangulated. It is especially important to collect data from respondents who occupy different social locations or are likely to have divergent views. For example, in Chenault's (2004) research on the public housing community, she interviewed multiple members of the resident council, as well as representatives of the housing authority and HUD officials; observed and interacted with members of the resident council; and performed a content analysis of HUD documents. Observing different people at different times in different places is another form of triangulation. Approaching problems using different theoretical frames and analyzing the data using more than one technique are also ways of engaging in triangulation. It is usually reassuring when triangulation leads to corroborating evidence, although it is not the kiss of death where this is not the case (Creswell, 1998, p. 202).

Although I am a fan of triangulation and recommend using as many types of triangulation as possible, I caution against rejecting data and conclusions just because triangulation identified inconsistencies. What might ultimately lead to more insight into a setting is understanding why different participants give different accounts, different types of data lead to different conclusions, and multiple researchers disagree with each other. Triangulation is useful in field research for verification, but using it to try to determine what finding is "the truth" runs counter to some paradigmatic assumptions that underpin qualitative research.

One of several common methods that can generate data for triangulation is observation. Procedures for collecting detailed observations are presented in the next chapter.

Chapter Highlights

---

1. Gaining entrée is negotiated and renegotiated throughout the research process.

2. Key actors are individuals who act as guides or mentors to the field researcher.

3. Formal and informal gatekeepers control access to a setting and the availability of data within the setting.

4. Arrival in a field setting is often filled with stress, fear, mistakes, and insecurities.

5. Although informed consent is a goal of most field researchers, actually getting informed consent from everyone encountered in the field is problematic.

6. Trusting, reciprocal relationships are the basis of good field research.

7. Multiple researchers, multiple data sources, multiple data types, and multiple theoretical approaches are all forms of triangulation.

8. Triangulation is important for ensuring the quality of the research.

Exercises

---

1.   Assume that you are interested in conducting an in-depth study of servers and customers in restaurants and that you would like to conduct your research in two restaurants that serve considerably different clientele. Develop an appropriate research question for your study. Then using a purposive sampling strategy, select two restaurants within driving distance. What strategy did you use? Why was it appropriate for your research? What restaurants did you select? Explain why you ultimately selected the two you did.

2.   Pretend that you want to conduct research to understand the day-to-day interactions in a funeral home. Discuss the procedures that you could use to gain the permission of the gatekeeper(s).

3.   Some field researchers strive for nonhierarchical relationships with participants, and deep friendships can develop. Do you think there are any circumstances when it is appropriate for a researcher to engage in a romantic relationship with a participant in the field? Would romantic attachments be appropriate after the fieldwork portion of the research is completed? Defend your answers.

4.   Select a setting of interest to you. Write approximately two pages describing procedures you can use for observing and interacting in this setting that include at least two types of triangulation.

6

Observations

Your paradigm has been decided, and you have theoretically grounded research questions. Field research is the tradition of inquiry you plan to use, and you have designed your methodology appropriately. At least preliminary access has been gained, and you have made a contact that might be able to help get you acclimated to the setting. Now is the time to immerse yourself in collecting data. The techniques used during data collection are called **methods**, the fourth component of the field research process. The method discussed in this chapter is observations.

Planning Observations

Observing functions as a major form of data collection for field research. Whereas obtaining members' accounts about activities within a setting through interviews and interactions is fundamental to field research, so too is seeing with one's own eyes. Of course, because researchers cannot always see everything in a setting, determine what is important to notice, and know the meanings of what they observed, even their firsthand accounts of observations will be partial and filtered.

When planning observations, field researchers consider several important questions:

1. Will the observations be covert or overt?

2. Will the researcher be participating in the setting or only observing?

3. Where and when will the observations occur?

4. Will the observations be structured or unstructured?

5. What will be observed? (Flick, 2002, pp. 137–149)

In keeping with the emergent design of field research, the answers to these questions might change during one's time in the field. As always, ethical issues and status characteristics affect what can be observed.

Covert or Overt Observations

As just noted, the first question one should answer when planning one's observations is whether the observations will be covert or overt. Because of the ethical concerns attached to covert research, this chapter focuses only on observations made during overt research.

As discussed in Chapter 2, the question of who should know they are being observed is not an easy one for the field researcher to answer. Frequent participants in a setting are fairly easily informed about the research. It is more difficult, however, to inform people that they are being observed when they enter and leave the scene fairly quickly.

Participating While Observing

A second question researchers face when they plan their observations involves whether they will participate in the setting, merely observe, or perhaps do a bit of both. The terms **participant** and **nonparticipant observations** indicate the degree to which the researcher actively participates in the field setting. The *participant observer* takes part in daily events while observing; the *nonparticipant observer* simply observes. To better understand the levels of involvement you might have as a field researcher, imagine a four-fold or four-celled table with one of the following components in each cell: *complete observer, observer as participant, participant as observer,* and *complete participant* (Gold, 1969; Junker, 1960). Each designation indicates the role researchers might play at any point in their research, and their primary role as either observer or participant determines their location within the table. On the basis of this classification system, during her dissertation research Chenault (2004) acted as *observer as participant*. Although she helped watch the children and serve food during events planned by the resident council in the public housing community, she did not actively participate in resident council meetings or suggest events the group could sponsor.

At times it is difficult to assign a categorical label to the researcher's level of involvement in a setting. For many researchers the degree of engagement is often highly variable, and the mere act of observing can function as a form of interacting because of its potential for reactivity. For example, during Bourgois's (1995) study of East Harlem, he routinely interacted with the residents—holding numerous conversations, shopping where they did—because he was a resident of the neighborhood. During these periods of observation, then, he was a complete participant. At other times, such as when he conducted observations in crack houses, his role as a participant was much smaller. He did not use crack, but his physical presence might have affected others' behaviors.

Another problem with a classification system is that what researchers think they are doing does not necessarily mesh with how participants interpret their activities (Warren & Karner, 2005). Although as a part of his research Van Maanen (1988) had attended the police academy, he was not a police officer so he could not officially participate in their activities. Yet, some of the officers incorporated him into their lives beyond his role as a researcher by giving him responsibilities that only police officers should perform. For example, some of the officers expected him to "watch their backs," as other officers would have done. Also, members of the public often assumed he was a plain-clothes detective (Van Maanen, 1988).

The decision whether to participate or observe, or perhaps do some of both, is affected by the paradigm and the tradition of inquiry being used. A researcher who employs a positivist paradigm might be more inclined than researchers using other paradigms toward merely observing. The researcher who engages in an ethnographic study is more likely to participate in a setting than one conducting evaluation research. Of course, one's research questions also will have a large influence on the level of participation. Rather then get mired in debates over classification systems or how much participation versus observation is required by each paradigm and tradition of inquiry, researchers planning fieldwork should make at least preliminary decisions about their role in the setting without worrying which label to attach to it.

With that said, arguably most field researchers actively engage in frequent interactions in the setting. Thus, embedded in this chapter, and in the chapters that follow on interviewing and writing field notes, is the notion that data are collected while the researcher is actively involved in the routine and not-so-routine events of everyday life in the setting.

Observation Boundaries

A third decision to be made by researchers involves where the observations will be conducted. Setting aside, for now, ethical and sampling issues, the answer to this question is both simple and complex. At times, the setting of interest has clear boundaries, such as a classroom, that limit where observations will be done. However, the boundaries of a setting are not always so clear; in fact, when a social group crosses many settings the lines of demarcation for observing can be highly amorphous. For example, when Duneier (1999) studied the men and women who were street vendors on Sixth Avenue, his observations were not confined to one place. He also observed the men as they salvaged for magazines and at the police station, where one of them went to pick up his belongings (p. 256). However, he did not observe the men when they were doing things in other places that were mostly unrelated to their activities as street vendors.

Structured and Unstructured Observations

Fourth, the researcher must decide if the observations will be structured, unstructured, or a combination of both, which is often the case. Both structured and unstructured observations are systematic and rigorous. The major difference is the amount of planning involved.

Highly structured observations usually have a well-defined observation guide and are scheduled for specific times. Sampling procedures might be used to determine observation times or people and events to be observed. The focus and location of the observations are predetermined. A researcher engaged in structured observations will not ignore important events outside the realm of their guide; however, he or she will concentrate on predetermined targets during the observations.

The format, purpose, and structure of observation guides vary. One type of observation guide uses questions to focus the observations. Wilson (2005) created such a guide for observing special and general education co-teachers in a general education class that included students with disabilities. Wilson's guide directed the observations in three major domains—meaning roles for each teacher, strategies of each student, and indicators of success (see Figure 6.1). Within each domain, a series of questions guided the observations.

How can I determine if a co-taught collaborative inclusion class is being taught as effectively as possible?

Questions I should be asking myself as I observe. . .

I. The Basics: Meaningful Roles for Each Teacher

1. Can the role of each teacher be defined at any given point in the lesson?
2. Is each role meaningful? Does each role enhance the learning process?
3. Do the teachers vary their roles during the course of the lesson?
4. Is each teacher well suited to the role(s) he or she is assuming?
5. Are both teachers comfortable with process AND content?
6. Is the special education teacher working with all students?

II. Strategies to Promote Success for ALL Students

1. What evidence is there that teachers engaged in co-planning the lesson?
2. Are the teachers focusing on process as well as content? Are they reinforcing important skills?
3. Are directions clear?
4. What strategies/modifications are being employed to assist struggling students?
5. What adaptations were made to materials in order to help struggling students complete tasks?
6. What strategies are being used to actively engage students?
7. How are students being grouped? Does it fit the task? Is it purposeful?
8. What reinforcement strategies are being employed?

III. Evidence of Success

1. Are struggling students answering/asking questions?
2. Are students engaged in meaningful work throughout the period?
3. How are teachers assessing the learning of each student?
4. What evidence is there that all students have been appropriately challenged?

Figure 6.1   Example of a Structured Observation Guide

SOURCE: From "This doesn't look familiar! A supervisor's guide for observing co-teachers." *Intervention in School and Clinic, 40* (p. 273) by G. Wilson, 2005. Reprinted with permission of Pro-Ed, Inc.

Unstructured observations, in contrast, are more flexible. This does not mean that unstructured observations are haphazard with no forethought. For example, researchers make sure that they observe at different times. The importance of this should be obvious; no doubt you can easily think of settings in which the dynamics vary widely over the course of the day, week, month, or year. Unstructured observations do not preclude focused attention on particular facets of a setting. However, researchers are less likely to have an observation guide, concentrating instead on what is deemed relevant as events unfold.

What paradigm is used can influence the type of observations employed. Structured observations are more common within a positivist paradigm than they are within other paradigms. However, researchers from all paradigms might conduct both structured and unstructured observations. Researchers also mix structured and unstructured observations throughout their time in the field.

Focus of Observations

The fifth question to be answered is what should be observed. Spradley (1980) provides excellent recommendations for guiding your observations during the early phases of your research. He suggests that you be able to describe nine features that appear in almost all social situations:

1. *Spaces:* the physical places

2. *Objects:* the physical things that are present

3. *Actors:* the people involved

4. *Act:* single actions that people do

5. *Activity:* a set of related acts people do

6. *Event:* a set of related activities that people carry out

7. *Time:* the sequencing that takes place over time

8. *Goals:* the things people are trying to accomplish

9. *Feelings:* the emotions felt and expressed. (p. 78)

Some of these features might require that you interact with the participants, not just observe them. For example, emotions *expressed* are observable; emotions *felt* usually require talking to someone.

As you continue to learn about field research in general, you will discover that describing even a single feature, such as space, can be a daunting task—but the really difficult part is yet to come. Observations should also include describing the intersection among the combinations of these features. For example, you should be able to describe how actors change over time, which actors are involved in activities, and what goals are associated with various events (Spradley, 1980, p. 83).

How and which things get observed will change over the course of the research. When first arriving in the field, researchers might engage in the type of observations Spradley (1980) suggests and then, as their research questions and interest in a setting become clearer, they might narrow their focus. Finally, highly selective observations are conducted (Flick, 2002, p. 140).

Prior to giving more concrete suggestions about observing, I want to clarify what I mean by the term. When most of us think of observing, we tend to think of an act that involves primarily—if not exclusively—the eyes. Watching is certainly an important part of collecting data in a field setting, but listening, smelling, touching, and tasting factor into the process. Also, as you are recording what you can see, don't forget to notice what you *cannot*. For example, temperature is not directly seen but has important implications for behavior.

Building upon the work of Spradley (1980), I focus on only three targets for observations: physical surroundings (space and objects), participants, and a summary category I call "actions." From the level of detail I provide on these three, no doubt you will realize that observing all the other items from Spradley's list—acts, activities, events, time, goals, and feelings—is equally difficult. Yet, it is these rigorous observations that elevate field research methodology above that which is accomplished by a casual observer. The data collected during your observations will be a major component of your analysis. When you enter the setting, your first goal is to consider your physical surroundings.

Observations of Physical Surroundings

Visiting the home of a new acquaintance can tell you a lot about the person. Simply by taking a quick look around, you can usually tell if the person is a music fan, a sports devotee, or a world traveler. A 35-inch television in the center of the room suggests something different about the person's television viewing patterns than would a 19-inch one tucked away in the corner. Our surroundings reflect a great deal about who we are.

Not surprising, field researchers pay a great deal of attention to physical surroundings. Spradley (1980) lists objects and space as key features of almost all social settings. The social implications of the physical surroundings rather than the surroundings themselves are of primary importance to the field researcher.

Size

Observations might begin with documenting the size of the setting—but they don't stop there. It would be singularly uninteresting for me to tell you that I know a room on your campus that measures 40 feet by 60 feet. The room dimensions become meaningful only when we understand the social significance of this amount of space. For example, space is often used as an indicator of social status. A room this size might indicate high social status if it served as the office of the athletic director, but it might indicate low prestige if it served as home for the entire Theatre Department. When field researchers observe physical surroundings, they hope to understand the implications of them for the social world. Highly detailed descriptive accounts aid the search for meaning.

Lighting

If you are engaging in systematic observations, note the *lighting*, a factor that conveys a great deal of social meaning. Think, for example, of how a flick of the lights during a theatrical production indicates that intermission is over. Is the lighting soft and subdued, bright and cold, inadequate, or designed to draw attention to or from something? What kind of atmosphere does the lighting convey? Does it affect how individuals in the setting interact with each other?

Color

Color is also used to create a mood, so it should be included in your observations. Are the colors neutral or do they tend to be bold? Are they soft and soothing? Are they well coordinated or do they seem haphazard? What purpose might they serve? Do the colors make you feel safe or anxious? For example, a graduate student told me that when she visited my office, its color—I refer to it as "dusty rose"—made her feel like she was inside a bottle of Pepto Bismol. I enjoyed this description, but of course it was not the ambiance for which I was shooting. In fact, I had painted it this color as a minor rebellious act against the standardization of institutional blue and beige. This is an instance of the importance of recording not only your assessment of the physical surroundings, but those of the participants as well.

Sounds

Also take note of the background *sounds*. Is the space full of laughter, sounds of machinery, piped-in music, telephones, or silence? How are changes in sounds tolerated; do people react quickly to changes or are they ignored? Are sounds used to summon individuals and convey information? The tones used on airplanes to discreetly signal flight attendants provide an example of such a secret system. Again, begin to record your impressions early. Like our sense of smell, our ability to notice sounds changes with exposure, so take note of the background sounds throughout your stay in a setting.

Objects

Pay close attention to the *objects* in the space: plants, furniture, books, tools, storage units, and so forth. Are the objects primarily functional or decorative? Are they in excellent, good, or poor condition? Do some objects make political statements? What do the objects indicate about status? What atmosphere do they seem to convey? For example, consider the difference between a sign in a business that says "The customer is always right" and one that says "We reserve the right to refuse service to anyone."

Smells

When you are making observations, don't forget to use all of your senses. The *smell* of the setting is important, too. Is the smell clean even though it might not look it, or vice versa? Are there scents and perfumes? Does it smell new or old? Can you smell the presence of pets, children, food, leather, oil, laundry, or chemicals? Does it have the scent of romance, family, or business? Report smells early, preferably upon your initial entry into the setting. Over time your nose will adjust or adapt to environmental odors, and your reaction to them will become less pronounced. If you wait, your ability to reproduce your initial response also can diminish. In contrast, though, in some settings, your sense of smell might become more acute with time. Since in any new setting you will not know in which situation your nose might find itself—getting used to the odors or smelling them more acutely—record your initial reactions and continue to do so throughout your observations.

When David Fetterman (1989) was conducting research among the Bedouins, he encountered odors that by Western standards might be considered bad. Fortunately, as a skilled field researcher, he was more concerned with developing and maintaining good field relations than he was with conforming to or being hampered by Western prejudices regarding good and bad smells. He relates,

> During my stay with the Bedouins, I tried not to let my bias for Western hygiene practices and monogamy surface in my interactions or writings. I say *tried* because my reaction to one of my first acquaintances, a Bedouin with a leathery face and feet, was far from neutral. I was astonished. I admired his ability to survive and adapt in a harsh environment, moving from one water hole to the next throughout the desert. However, my personal reaction to the odor of his garments (particularly after a camel ride) was far from impartial. He shared his jacket with me to protect me from the heat. I thanked him, of course, because I appreciated the gesture and did not want to insult him. But I smelled like a camel for the rest of the day in the dry desert heat. I thought I didn't need the jacket because we were only a kilometer or two from our destination, Saint Catherine's monastery, but the short trip took forever— up rocky paths and down through *wadis* or valleys. I learned later that without his jacket I would have suffered from sunstroke. The desert heat is so dry that perspiration evaporates almost immediately, and an inexperienced traveler does not always notice when the temperature climbs above 130 degrees Fahrenheit. By slowing down the evaporation rate, the jacket helped me retain water. Had I rejected his jacket and, by implication, Bedouin hygiene practices, I would have baked, and I would never have understood how much their lives revolve around water, the desert's most precious resource. Our seemingly circuitous ride followed a hidden water route, not a straight line to the monastery. (p. 33)

If you undertake field research for a class assignment, chances are good that you will not find yourself in a position as precarious as Fetterman's. However, this example is illustrative for two reasons. First, it demonstrates how smell—something we might ordinarily take for granted—played a crucial role in Fetterman's observations. More important, it reinforces the point that at the heart of field research is the concern for social relationships. Regardless of what one is observing, one should privilege such relationships. Not only did Fetterman's concern for his relationship with the Bedouin lead to a better understanding of desert culture, it also literally saved his life.

This section offers only a few suggestions about how to put all of your senses to use when you observe in the physical world. Because physical surroundings are less apt to change than the participants, intense observations of them are front-loaded: The strongest impressions most likely will arrive early in the experience. However, you will still have to watch for changes to occur over time.

Observations of Participants

You will spend most of your time as a field researcher observing the people in the setting, witnessing their interactions with each other and the physical world, and joining them in a variety of activities. Although each setting might contain a core set of participants, your observations should include nonmembers who might only briefly enter the scene or interact with the regular participants.

Physical Characteristics

Begin your observations of participants in a setting by noticing their status characteristics. On the surface, this sounds like a relatively easy task: You note the gender, race, and approximate age of the people being observed. However, do not let your personal experiences deceive or prejudice you. When I first visited Nicaragua, for example, I consistently estimated children's ages as much younger than they were and the adults' ages as much older. Initially, I had failed to realize that the poverty of the people had greatly affected the usual physical signs by which I estimate age, such as height. Observation of an individual's appearance is not limited to race, gender, and age, however. Nearly every feature of the individual is potentially important.

Dress, hairstyle, and other personal adornments also convey meaning and have implications. People react to others' appearances, sometimes in negative ways. For example, a graduate student in my department changed his hairstyle to reduce the number of racist remarks yelled at him from passing cars as he walked around town. Although the risks are not as high for everyone, he is not alone in presenting himself in a particular way to try to manage the reaction of others. In a situation such as this, one would not know through observations why the student changed his hair; however, a good field researcher would record the change and make a note to discuss it with him when appropriate.

Observe personal symbols used in a setting. In addition to including descriptions of cultural symbols in your field notes, try to determine their social significance for participants. I remember when having a tattoo implied that someone was a "certain type" of person. Now, what might be meaningful about a tattoo is what it represents or where it is located, not whether one has one. Record symbols even if you aren't sure if they have any social significance. As you learn more about a setting, you might be pleased that you wisely recorded details that at the time had little meaning for you. Once such physical descriptions are recorded, move to considering how individuals in the setting speak to each other, either openly or through body language.

Behaviors

Most observations are of behaviors: who arrives, who goes, and who does what with whom, when, and how. Routine activities, special events, random behaviors, and unanticipated happenings are carefully documented. Whereas writing a descriptive account of behaviors is relatively easy, the goal for many field researchers is not merely to describe but to understand. Again, immersion in the field setting helps the researcher assess the meanings behind behaviors. Because behaviors are often the "meat" of field research, they are discussed in considerable detail later in this guide.

Body Language

One thing that can help your understanding involves paying close attention to *body language,* an extremely important part of communication. Which facial expressions are used in certain situations? How do people stand in relationship to each other? What is their posture? How much space do they take up—expansive or small relative to their size? How do they move; do they appear confident or unsure? How much eye contact do they maintain and for how long? Who is touching whom in what context? Does the body language change as individuals enter and leave a setting, or does it vary by the status characteristics of the participants? Observing the minutiae of body language is not an easy task, but when done effectively it provides insights that go well beyond what people say openly to each other.

Verbal Behaviors

Verbal behaviors function as another major category of observations. By verbal behavior, I am referring to more than just what was said. Field researchers often record the text of conversations verbatim to retain the grammatical and syntactical choices of the speakers. However, field researchers are also aware that talk is not objective reporting of factual data. Rather, talk also is part of, not independent of, the social world, so the field researcher explores the way verbal accounts are used to create meaning within the context of social relationships (Emerson, 1988). The section on interviewing will offer more information about the importance of talk.

Speech Patterns

To help understand the talk within the larger setting, pay attention to the characteristics of *speech patterns* used by participants. Which types of words are being used during the conversations? For example, are slang words, swear words, or technical words used regularly? Does the setting have an argot (words and meanings specific to that setting)? I was totally confused why undergraduates were saying "word" in what seemed to me to be odd occasions until someone told me its alternative meanings—agreement, affirmation, informal greeting, and a substitute for "really."

Pay attention to who does most of the talking and whose suggestions are followed, as well as whose are rejected or ignored. Who interrupts and who doesn't is worthy of note. What do these behaviors tell you about power and status rankings in this setting?

You can gather hints of embedded meaning by listening to the tone of a conversation. Is it polite, hostile, relaxed, instrumental, playful, or formal? Are voices soft or loud, modulated or monotone? Remember that *how* something is said frequently is as important as *what* is said. Your descriptive account of talk should include not just the words, but also the tone, implied meaning, body language used when speaking, and a host of other factors.

Although tape-recording is the preferred method for capturing speech, even that falls short in some settings, making field notes extremely important. For example, Bourgois (1995) noted that much of the speech of the men in "El Barrio" had a performance dimension. He writes, "Without the complex, stylized punctuation provided by body language, facial expression, and intonation, many of the transcribed narratives of crack dealers appear flat, and sometimes even inarticulate, on the written page" (p. 341). I highly suspect that Bourgois had detailed notes to supplement the transcripts.

Thus far, I have discussed observations of physical space and objects, as well as nonverbal and some verbal behavior of members—probably the easiest of the common features of social situations identified by Spradley (1980). Unfortunately, these attributes only scratch the surface of what occurs in the social world. Field researchers want to know what people *do:* How do they go about doing the things they do, why are they doing these things, and how do they feel about doing them? And then, field researchers seek understanding of the meanings attached to the actions and events. Field researchers seek answers to these sorts of questions, a result made possible through rigorous observations.

Observations of Actions

Observing activities, acts, events, time sequencing, goals, and feelings requires the researcher to focus on the behaviors of individuals—usually more than one at a time—as well as on the features already discussed. Because these features constitute the "stuff" of everyday life in the setting, plan to produce rigorous and detailed observations of them. After all, they might end up being crucial to your analysis, and you might want to include such thick descriptions in your final manuscript.

If you plan to undertake fieldwork, you can sharpen your observation skills by breaking them down into the domains suggested by Spradley (1980). When in a setting, ask yourself key questions. What event is occurring? What is one activity that is part of the event? What is one act that contributes to this activity? What is another act that contributes to this activity? In what order are the acts occurring? Who is engaging in each act? What are the observers of the acts or activities doing? Continue with similar questions, one after the other, each time observing and documenting your observations and thoughts.

As the observer, avoid letting yourself become like a voice-activated tape recorder or a motion-detector light, otherwise sleeping objects that activate only when they sense sound or movement. When someone speaks or moves, the field researcher writes down text, simultaneously observing body language, and so forth. When the action stops, does he or she then take a break and wait for someone in the setting to throw the "on" switch? Definitely not. Try to always be "on." Even when nothing seems to be happening, strive to be aware and analytical. For example, in a study of suburban community, it is as important to note who is not working in their yards on Saturday morning as it is to note who is.

The importance of actively observing nonaction is probably not a new concept for you. You might have been trained in art classes to look at the negative spaces formed by objects in addition to the objects themselves, or you might have heard the saying "not making a decision is making a decision." However, many of us are used to only subconsciously noticing the background while consciously reacting to the foreground. In fact, in many settings the background is purposely obscured. During a play, for example, lighting changes help create mood changes, but the audience is supposed to notice only the change in the mood—not the lighting per se. Field researchers combat the tendency to observe only the foreground; it is important to observe both background and foreground but also seek to determine how they work together. Otherwise, we run the risk of paying attention only to high-status members, because in most settings not all group members have equal access to center stage. Field researchers are well aware that those in the background complete much of the important work in a setting.

Ethics

As with the other aspects of field research, ethics is a concern during observations. When you are observing, do so ethically. Avoid sneaking into areas designated as off-limits to outsiders or wandering into places to which you have not been granted access. Even if you have been given permission to enter a particular space, this does not mean you have free license to observe everything there. For example, if you are observing the secretarial staff in a department, this does not mean it is acceptable for you to go through desk drawers without explicit permission to do so. Engaging in field research is not a justification for observing private behaviors, places, or things. However, often you can appropriately ask what is behind closed doors, what is kept in file cabinets, and what sorts of things participants have in their desks drawers. You simply cannot look without permission.

Summary

At the beginning of your research, you have the almost overwhelming task of observing everything simultaneously. Since the task can be so daunting, you might be tempted into selectivity. Remember, however, that assuming you will know what is important to observe and what can be ignored is risky, particularly at the beginning of your research. Always err on the side of documenting more than what you think is important. As your research progresses, your understanding grows, and your goals become more specific, your observations will become more focused.

In addition to observations and informal interactions in the field, researchers often hold interviews with participants in the setting. Three types of interviews are presented in the next chapter.

Chapter Highlights

1. Observations can be covert or overt.

2. Field researchers participate in varying degrees in the setting.

3. Researchers need to decide what areas, objects, people, and events should be included in the observations.

4. Observations can be highly structured, with observation guides and predetermined schedules for observing.

5. Field researchers use all their senses during observations.

6. Field researchers observe the physical surroundings, the people, and the verbal and nonverbal behaviors that occur in a setting.

Exercises

1.   Paul Atkinson and Martyn Hammersley wrote the following: "*All* social research is a form of participant observation, because we cannot study the social world without being part of it" (1994, p. 249). What do you think they mean by this statement? What are the implications of their statement for those who classify field research on the basis of the level of participation? Do you agree or disagree with Atkinson and Hammersley's statement? Justify your answers.

2.   Go to a setting where you have not been before. Take notes while you observe for 15 minutes. After typing your notes, compare your descriptions with the categories suggested by Spradley (1980, p. 78)—space, actor, activities, objects, acts, events, time, goals, and feelings. Do your notes include descriptions of all nine categories? Are your notes for some categories more complete than others? Reflect on what you have learned by completing this exercise.

3.   Spend 15 minutes in two different locations. Take notes on the sounds of each place, including periods of silence, in as much detail as possible. For example, saying that you hear someone walking is not sufficient. Rather, describe the sounds made by the person walking. Do not include the content of what is being said in your descriptions. Write a descriptive account that focuses on the sounds of each place.

7

Interviews

In addition to making detailed observations and keeping notes on conversations with participants, field researchers collect verbal data through interviews. In this chapter, I am making a distinction between interviews and talk that occurs in the course of everyday events in a setting. In both cases, the field researcher may be involved. However, in an interview, the field researcher asks questions for the purpose of seeking information directly related to the research. This may or may not be the case with questions that the researcher might ask at any given moment during routine interactions.

Although speaking with others comes easily to some of us, interviews conducted for the purposes of field research require some practice, as well as the ability to adapt to changing settings and situations. This section of the chapter provides you with more than a few suggestions on the process of interviewing. Please keep in mind that the advice it offers might not apply to countries other than the United States of America. As Kvale (1996) appropriately reminds us, "In other cultures, different norms may hold for interactions with strangers concerning initiative, directness, openness, and the like" (p. 127). Even within the United States, the advice offered here might have to be modified depending on the group you choose to study.

The three types of interviews most often used by field researchers are **unstructured, structured,** and **semistructured.**

Unstructured Interviews

Unstructured or **informal interviews** are similar to conversations. Indeed, researchers are often given the advice to make an unstructured interview like a conversation—and certainly one can morph into the other. One distinction is that during an unstructured interview, interaction between the participant and the field researcher targets primarily the interests of the researcher; this is not necessarily the case during a conversation. However, because of the overlap between the two, at various points this chapter will blend the discussions of unstructured interviews and conversations. As I describe unstructured interviews, you will no doubt notice their highly variable nature. Although you should not expect that "anything goes," unstructured interviews—compared to other types—have considerable flexibility in how they are held and possess relatively few guidelines.

Unstructured interviews involve little standardization. The first question asked of one interviewee might differ totally from the first question asked of the next interviewee. Indeed, rarely will interviewees be asked the same questions. A field researcher might ask one participant a single question and ask another person many questions. Rather than being planned, an unstructured interview evolves.

During an unstructured interview, the interviewee is given fairly free range to talk about any aspect related to the broad interests of the researcher, as long as he or she does not stray too long or too far from what the researcher thinks is important. Since researchers often come to understand what is useful to them only during analysis, giving a wide latitude to respondents can result in very fruitful caches of information.

Whereas generally you are able to allot a fixed amount of time to more structured interviews, unstructured interviews can last from a few minutes to a few hours—and rarely will you be able to estimate the time in advance. Furthermore, field researchers can indeed schedule an unstructured interview, but they often take place spontaneously.

Unstructured interviews are not equally distributed: Some participants might be interviewed many times, others only once or a few times, and some participants not at all. Sometimes an unstructured interview begins between just the field researcher and one participant, but then others join in. In fact, the interview might continue long after the original participant has left the setting.

Informal interviews are not about structure and hierarchy but about talking and mutual discovery (Neuman, 1991, p. 367). An unstructured interview can be a reciprocal process, with the researcher and the participant in the setting engaging in a dialogue. In such a situation, field researchers can be expected not only to ask questions, but also to answer them. Both researcher and participant share feelings, impressions, ideals, and information. An unstructured interview often goes where it wants to go and is affected by the context in which it occurs.

I agree with Fontana and Frey that informal interviews are shaped more by "give and take" and "empathic understanding" than by a series of rules that must be followed. They argue that this approach to interviewing is more "honest, morally sound, and reliable, because it treats the respondent as an equal, allows him or her to express personal feelings, and therefore presents a more 'realistic' picture than can be uncovered using traditional interview methods" (1994, p. 371). At the same time, I know that this view is idealistic. In reality, a "give and take" interview style does not guarantee fruitful information.

Although this notion of mutual discovery is consistent with the epistemological belief of an interpretive paradigm, most interviews will not consist of analytical insights and profound truths. In many cases, they will be about mundane things unrelated to the research. Sometimes, in fact, interview responses won't even make sense. One cannot always be sure why that is the case. Maybe we missed the point because we were not paying attention, or we don't know the argot being used; maybe the speaker communicated the point badly; or maybe the speaker isn't sure what the point of the talk is. An interviewee can be unsure, equivocal, ambiguous, confused, or unaware of how, when, where, and why things happened. Van Maanen warns us that it is fairly routine for interviews to be obscured in some "existential fog" (1982, p. 141).

At the same time, field researchers take care not to dismiss too soon talk that seems irrelevant. For example, in the early days of their research experiences, graduate students often claim that their interviewee did not tell them what they wanted to know. Of course, I remind them that if they already know it, then their research is not necessary, and they should search for another topic. In most cases, students get the not-so-subtle hint and work harder to remain open during future interviews.

Still, field researchers probably have more interviews that fall flat than they have successful ones. For example, Van Maanen (1982) relates the response he received when he attempted to talk with one police officer in the field:

> I don't have nothing to say to you and you don't have nothing to say to me, I'm putting in my time. I've got a year to go until I pull the pin and I don't want any trouble. I don't know what you want and I wouldn't give a s___ even if I did. You mind your business and I'll mind mine. (p. 111)

Although this response might sound rather hostile, actually it was one of his friendlier rejections. As a field researcher, be prepared for such rejections and try to steel yourself not to take them personally. Simply respect people's wishes not to be interviewed.

When you first begin conducting informal interviews, you might ask what are known as "grand tour questions," those you hope will be answered with a broad overview of the setting or the participant's life (Fetterman, 1989). For example, you might ask, "What are all those people doing?" This question might result in an impromptu tour—and an interview that continues on the move. Asking a participant of the setting to show you around allows you to start learning where things are, what things are called, and what is important—at least to the person giving the tour. After that, the role of the interviewer is to provide responses or ask further questions designed to encourage the interviewee to continue talking.

Fairly soon after we started our research on health care in Midsouth County, my colleagues and I asked a general question about transportation. We learned that some of the women were too poor to have cars. Because of this, the women often had to take taxis, a service paid for by Medicaid, to get to medical appointments. This information led to an impromptu conversation with a taxi driver. He explained that some taxi drivers were able to boost their incomes by encouraging women to visit hospitals and clinics in another county. Those drivers who did so were able to accomplish their goals by perpetuating the rumor that local health services were not as good as those available in other counties, which led to mistrust and avoidance of local services by the women. If this was indeed the case, then it might be one of the factors leading to no care, delays in health care, underuse of local services, and increased costs to taxpayers. When we started our research, we had not thought about pursuing the implications of Medicaid-reimbursed travel, but the topic arose out of our first informal interviews. When we later talked to public health officials, we included questions about transportation in our structured interview guide.

Structured Interviews

Structured interviews also play important roles in field research. Unlike unstructured interviews, the researcher conducting a structured interview asks, in specific order, precise questions of interest to him or her. He or she may even plan the **probes** in advance and take care to ask each question of each interviewee in the same way. During the structured interview, then, the interviewer determines the questions, controls their order and pace, and tries to keep the respondent on track; otherwise, he or she does not actively participate. Additionally, structured interviews usually are scheduled for a particular time and place and are expected to take a specific amount of time. Clearly, the structured interview possesses more guidelines than its unstructured cousin.

Training for structured interviews usually involves learning a series of don'ts. For example:

1. Don't deviate from the standard explanation of the study.

2. Don't deviate from the sequence of questions or question wording.

3. Don't give the interviewee any of your personal views.

4. Don't interpret the meaning of a question or give clarifications.

5. Don't improvise by adding answer categories or making word changes. (Fontana & Frey, 1994, p. 362)

When I was in graduate school, I received specific training on how to avoid answering questions during structured interviews. When interviewees asked us questions, we were taught to say things such as "I'm here to learn your opinion, not to give mine." Flexibility is not a key feature of structured interviews.

Even in structured interviews, you cannot simply dissociate yourself and forget that maintaining good social relationships still plays an important role. In my experience, interviewees often will ask, "Is that all right?" or say, "I hope I'm giving you what you want." I think reassuring them about their helpfulness and encouraging them to answer however they want is important. I do not have preplanned statements for such situations. Certainly, too, my body language will vary from interviewee to interviewee. I hope that during all interviews I smile, nod, look concerned, and make sounds that appropriately indicate I am engaged in the interaction. Although I ask the same questions, I have no illusion that my verbal and nonverbal behavior is standardized. Just because interviews are structured does not mean that as interviewers we must become machines that simply ask questions and record responses.

Structured interviews are particularly useful for comparing answers from different groups of respondents. For example, the same structured interview about masculinity could be held with undergraduate male college students enrolled in both male-dominated and female-dominated majors (A. LoMascolo, personal communication, December 13, 2005). After analyzing the responses of each group, the researcher could then compare the results. Under some conditions, as well, structured interview data are amenable to being transformed into quantitative data and analyzed using statistical techniques. For example, responses to some questions can be organized such that frequencies and nonparametric tests of statistical significance can be calculated and reported (Miles & Huberman, 1994).

Semistructured Interviews

Field researchers who enjoy some level of flexibility regarding how an interview is administered but who wish to maintain some structure over its parameters might prefer a semistructured interview. In a semistructured interview, the interviewer uses an interview guide with specific questions that are organized by topics but are not necessarily asked in a specified order. The flow of the interview, rather than the order in a guide, determines when and how a question is asked. Depending on how the interview progresses, a question previously planned for late in the interview might be asked earlier. Additionally, interviewees often answer a question before it is asked. If so, the question is skipped.

Semistructured interviews are usually scheduled in advance and expected to last a certain amount of time; during them, the interviewer might engage in dialogue with the interviewee, rather than simply ask questions, particularly if an interpretive or critical paradigm frames the research.

This was the case for Rosemary Ellis (2002) who, for her master's thesis, conducted interviews with women who self-mutilated. Ellis had engaged in this practice herself and made this clear to the women she interviewed. As a result of this connection, some of the expected hesitancy of taking part in an interview on a sensitive topic was reduced, and the resulting interviews were lively and rich in detail. Ellis had predetermined questions organized by topic, but she did not ask these in the same order and sometimes varied the wording of the questions. During the interviews, which mostly took the form of dialogues, Ellis and these women compared stories and asked each other questions. Despite its appeal, though, the interactive nature of semistructured interviews is not without its problems. Upon listening to the tape of her first interview, Ellis had no recourse but to laugh at herself when she realized she did most of the talking.

Selecting the Appropriate Type of Interview

One's particular configuration of paradigm, tradition of inquiry, research questions, purpose of research, analytic strategy, and a host of other factors will help determine which interview type one should use. Those who situate their work within a positivist paradigm tend to prefer the structured interview. Field researchers who use an interpretive paradigm often lean toward semistructured and unstructured interviews. Sometimes, researchers alternate interview types. For example, an evaluation researcher might begin his or her project with an unstructured interview and then later move to semistructured and even to highly structured interviews. What analysis strategy will be used to answer the research questions and the organization of the final manuscript can affect the type of interview that should be used, and vice versa. After all, field research is not a set of linear steps.

In my experience on graduate committees, the most contentious issue during proposal defenses is what type of interview the graduate student should use. If the student has not clearly established the paradigm, the research questions, and the analytical strategy, or if a committee member refuses to accept any paradigm other than his or her own, then an academic struggle occurs. On one hand, the student is asked, *How are you going to compare answers if not everyone is asked the same question?* On the other hand, the question is, *How can you say that your work is based on the perspectives of the participants in the setting when you limit what can be said by using such highly structured questions?* If you are conducting field research for a graduate degree, ask yourself how you would answer these two questions before you select the type of interview you will use. If you are conducting interviews as an undergraduate student, your worries in this arena are fewer: Your instructor can help guide you toward the most appropriate interview type.

Choosing the type of interview you conduct, however, is simply the first step in the process. Good interviews require practice. Before undertaking your first real interview, conduct pilot interviews. Enlist your friends, roommates, family members, and neighbors as interviewees. Seek feedback. Practice again. Although memorizing your questions is not necessary, you should be able to ask them with only minimal glancing at the interview guide. Remember that the more you maintain eye contact with the respondent, the better, so rather than becoming obsessed with your next question, try engaging with the person across from you.

Question Construction

Although the questions themselves should never become the sole focus of your efforts and attention, certainly they are central features of any good interview. Consistent with the research questions, interview questions often are "what" and "how" questions: *What happened after you left the classroom? How did you find out? How do you decide who gets to attend? What was the most important reason for wanting to leave? How did you feel when that happened?* "What" and "how" questions are often easy and interesting for the participants to answer and frequently are useful for eliciting detailed responses that can lend insight to your research questions (Kvale, 1996).

Interview questions sometimes start, however, with other query words, such as "have," "do," "could," and "can." You should take care that these questions are asked in a tone that suggests that more than a one-word answer is expected, unless this is what you want. For example, the question, *Have you ever been required to do a peer evaluation for a group project?* could be answered with a "yes" or "no." If the goal is to determine what students felt about conducting a peer evaluation, the question should be rephrased.

Unless a single-word response is sufficient, devise questions that elicit additional commentary, particularly from individuals who are hesitant to talk. This is where the *open-ended question* comes in handy— the question that prompts the extended sharing of information. Think, for example, of the question, *Do you like your social research methods class?* This *closed-ended question* can be answered only with a "yes" or a "no." Changing the question to open-ended—*What are some of the things you like about social research methods?*—is not likely to elicit a "yes" or "no," although in rare instances it might result in another one-word answer: *nothing.*

When creating questions, researchers also think about how much they want to constrain the range of possible answers (Flick, 2002). Compare the leeway the respondent would have with these three questions: *What was your childhood like? What do you recall about moving to Conway? What was more important to you at the time, the approval of your peers or your parents?* Interviews usually move from questions that impose few restrictions on the respondent to ones that require specific information (Flick, 2002).

One caution involves the use of "why" questions. Asking your interviewees "why" they did something might lead to discomfort from being put on the spot to come up with an explanation to justify their behavior

(Kvale, 1996). If they are unsure about their own motivations, they might feel compelled to create one. Further, "why" questions can sometimes sound confrontational. If the interviewer can ask the right "how" and "what" questions, then the reasons for and explanations of behavior may become clear during the analysis (Kvale, 1996).

Unlike research questions, interview questions should not contain academic jargon—phrases like *hegemonic masculinity, social capital,* and *alienation* that sound right at home in the former are definitely not in the latter. Thus, you probably will not ask research questions directly during the interview, and if you do, you often ask them toward the end.

Probes are another type of question often used by interviewers. A probing question encourages the interviewee to expand on an answer, to say more in response to the original question. A common probe question is, *Can you tell me more about that?* Often, probes are included on structured interview guides, so they should be as carefully planned as the original question.

A **follow-up question** is not preplanned, but the astute researcher hears the need for it. Interviewing requires active listening, not just asking questions. Although such questions are used more sparingly in structured interviews, active engagement allows researchers to ask follow-up questions that might end up being as important as any question in the original interview guide. The emerging design of qualitative research allows for an important follow-up question created during an interview to be asked of all subsequent interviewees. Alternatively, sometimes questions in the interview guide are dropped on the basis of ongoing analysis and information received from earlier interviewees.

Because of the importance of questions to a successful interview, there is no end to the useful advice that can be offered related to them. Good interview questions should be short and easily understood and should not contain multiple parts. Shorter questions lead to longer answers; you know you are in trouble during an interview if your questions are longer than the answers (Kvale, 1996). However, very short questions can also be vague, which can in turn lead to poor responses. Avoid the urge to end a question with the phrase "if so, why?" Let the respondent answer one question at a time. Any question that has the word "and" in it should be reviewed to ensure that it is not a "two-parter." Avoid beginning an interview with demographic questions, such as, *How old are you?* These might seem like safe questions for beginning an interview, but they are uninteresting to the respondent and lead to short answers— a pattern that then might be continued through the remainder of the interview. Finally, remember that one way to help determine if you have good questions is to practice asking them.

A carefully crafted interview can be worthless if you fail to ask yourself one important question: *Will the interview elicit useful information for answering my research questions?* To help ensure that is the case, engage in one last activity before considering your interview guide final. Match your interview questions with your research questions. I routinely have graduate students engage in this activity. After one such session, a student realized she had 10 questions that would help her answer her first research question, only one that applied to her second research question, and none for another research question. Quite a few of her questions were not relevant for any of her research questions, nor did they seem as though they would be useful to her analytically in other ways. After this exercise, she created a new interview guide. The lack of congruence between interview questions and research questions is common on early drafts, so I strongly recommend actively checking for correspondence.

Framing the Interview

With all of the work you put into devising your questions, do not forget that a good interview begins not with the questions, but with the care and nurturance of the relationship between the researcher and the person being interviewed. Thus, researchers should plan the time *before* the first question is asked with the same care they took when determining that question. First impressions matter.

Location of the Interview

The nature of fieldwork is such that the researcher does not have control over many aspects of the research. Thus, field researchers often have no choice about where or when an interview will be conducted. Indeed, an unstructured interview is often held while the participant is going about his or her daily tasks, as it then occurs naturally and does not impinge greatly upon the interviewee's time. However, semistructured and structured interviews are usually held in places carefully preselected.

Where an interview is held can affect its quality. As the researcher, you are responsible for thinking about convenience, distractions, and noise levels. The location should be convenient and comfortable for the interviewee, but letting participants decide where it is held is not always a good idea. For example, they might have become so attuned to the noises and activities of their daily lives that they no longer consider them potentially intrusive. As a result, they might select locations with too many distractions, such as children, phones, and televisions. The process of transcribing tapes—already time-consuming—becomes a nightmare when background noises obscure the participants' voices and make their statements unintelligible. If possible, prescreen locations to determine the level of activity and noise. By agreeing to the interview, some interviewees face tangible risks—emotional, economic, social, or physical—so you should take extreme care in selecting a location that will provide both comfort and safety.

Interview Courtesy

A respectful and appreciative tone during your interactions is only appropriate, because the participants are, after all, under no obligation to talk to you. In addition to engaging in the usual greetings, small talk, and sincere thanks, you might consider providing an overview of the purpose of the interview before you begin, as it is often useful for putting the participants at ease. You might, for example, begin by telling them your overarching research questions. Convey to them your interest in having them describe and explain the meanings of their experiences to you. Share your hope that they will find answering your questions a pleasant experience, a conversation rather than an inquisition. At this time, too, provide any special instructions or reassurances. For example, Lewis (2005) reminded the African American, urban males he was interviewing that they should not talk about any behaviors that could put them at risk—with the criminal justice system or otherwise. He made sure that they understood that if they did talk about such behaviors he would have to erase it from the tape and possibly stop the interview.

Write out what you plan to say and practice it before the interview. You might find that you are as nervous about holding the interview as your interviewee, so—again—practice ensures confidence. Once you are comfortable with your opening remarks, they will cease sounding rehearsed and instead flow naturally.

Ethics

Previous chapters have already discussed numerous ethical issues, many of which are relevant to the interviewing process. Nonetheless, it might be fruitful to reiterate some points about ethics—and offer a few more.

Rapport is often mentioned in textbooks as a necessary ingredient for conducting good interviews, and fieldwork more generally. Such textbooks even provide suggestions for developing rapport, some of which are included in this guide as well. Yet, I ask myself, as do others, at what point does using preconceived plans for developing rapport turn into manipulation of respondents—sort of like a good pick-up line (Fontana & Frey, 1994; Oakley, 1981)? Is it ethical to rely on gimmicks for facilitating rapport so that the interviewee will do what you want? Is complimenting them prior to the interview on their clothes—a technique that might make them feel good—a small social lie and therefore harmless or is it actually manipulative? In many social encounters, we are less than honest, and thank goodness we are. I do not want everyone I meet telling me I am having a bad hair day. Yet, because there are no ethical guidelines to cover such gray areas, I hope that field researchers reflect on the point at which nurturing a social relationship for the sake of a good interview becomes unethical manipulation of the interviewee.

Informed consent is obviously important to the interview process. No matter how slow or inaccurate you believe your note-taking skills to be, tape-recording interviews without explicit permission is unethical. It is not enough to inform a participant that you are going to tape-record and let them protest. Even if this information is included on the informed consent form that the interviewee has signed, verbally explain why you want to record the interview and then ask for permission before starting to record.

Another ethical concern involves sensitivity to the context in which an informal interview occurs. Being sensitive to the context means focusing on more than whether the setting will establish the stage for honest answers. What might be an ethical question in one setting might be unethical in another. That said, it is not necessarily unethical for researchers to ask for personal information or for a participant to disclose it under the right circumstances. However, be careful with personal topics so as not to cause the participants any harm, including emotional distress. Unfortunately, you often won't know whether an issue will be painful or sensitive for someone until it is too late. For example, I conducted an interview with a college student that included questions on family violence and eating disorders. The interview had lasted about an hour and had gone smoothly right up to the point where I asked her how many sisters she had. She broke into tears and cried for several minutes before regaining composure. Although in this case she reassured me that all she needed was a few tissues, I gave her the number of the campus counseling center and the number for a 24-hour crisis center. I never was able to figure out the source of her distress—and more importantly, I did not ask. As a field researcher, you need to be prepared for the unexpected and know when to, in the most basic of terms, back off.

Finally, during interviews field researchers need to be good listeners, but we also have to be careful not to promise, even if only implicitly, more than we can deliver. For example, most of us do not have the skills to be counselors, and we should avoid taking on that role (Fetterman, 1989). While we are collecting data in the field, we need to think carefully about the ethical implications of helping people explore problems—for example, family violence—and then leaving them without support once our research is completed. Prior to conducting interviews on sensitive topics, talk to your peers, instructors, experts, and anyone else you think can provide sound advice to help you avoid ethical mistakes. Further, for all interviews about topics that might be potentially distressful, you should have a list of resources with numbers that the respondent can call. The information should be on a handout that you can give to the participant.

Status Characteristics

Even when armed with solid questions and with a strong sense of ethical boundaries, one of the challenges the researcher faces involves interviewing someone who is essentially different from him or her—different gender, race, ethnicity, economic status, educational status, and so on. Most likely, an interviewee's status characteristics will differ from yours not just in one way, but in many ways. Faced with an awareness of the difficulties such interviews might bring, undergraduate and graduate students often ask, *Should I interview someone different from me? Would the interviews be any good?* They are not alone in asking this. Field researchers long have asked this question and, over time, the prevailing views have changed.

Those working within a positivist tradition once felt that if the interviewer was objective and neutral and used the proper demeanor to prompt the interviewee to talk freely, then any effect of status characteristics would be rendered moot. Although objectivity and value neutrality still play central roles within a positivist paradigm, rarely today will someone working within this tradition suggest that status characteristics are irrelevant. Certainly, those who frame their work within interpretive and critical frameworks assert that status characteristics very much matter.

Throughout this text, I have used the example of gender to discuss how status characteristics affect the field research process. Gender is important to interviewing as well. We know, for example, that during interviews with men, female interviewers sometimes experience sexual overtures, sexual harassment, or treatment as lower in status (Warren, 1988).

As with gender, race holds implications for field research. A young, White graduate student in class shared how she had trouble scheduling interviews with elderly Black males. When an older Black woman, who was also working on the project, made the initial phone calls, the men were quite agreeable. As it turns out, though, when the graduate student arrived to conduct the interviews, the men talked at length about their experiences. The nature of fieldwork is such that most likely the men would have told their stories differently had a Black male of their generation conducted the interviews, and the dynamics between yet another Black male and interviewees also would have resulted in different accounts. It would be difficult to predict in advance which of these interviews would result in the richer, more detailed interview, as similarities in race, gender, and age do not in and of themselves guarantee positive social interaction.

Rest assured, for successful research to occur, researcher and respondents need not match on key characteristics. If this were not the case, much important research would remain undone. Leibow (1994), for example, was not a homeless woman, yet his book provided valuable insights into the lives of women who were. Eric Klinenberg (2002) was not a victim of the disastrous heat wave in Chicago in 1995 that killed more than 500 people, yet he wrote a powerful ethnography on this tragedy. Katherine Newman's (1999) study of teenagers who work at "burger barns" in urban centers is another example of the lack of congruence between researcher and those in the setting. Anthropologists rarely share characteristics with participants of a setting.

I agree with those scholars who argue that active concern about social relationships is essential for reducing potential negative effects of dissimilarities between researcher and participants (Fontana & Frey, 1994). If during interviews we can close the social distance, however briefly, we might have a better chance of understanding each other.

Although I believe in the importance of good relationships and the possibility of creating them, I am not as much of a Pollyanna (Porter, 1913) as I might sound. Sometimes interviewees deliberately lie to us and have such strong feelings against us that they are uncooperative. An extremely troubling time for me occurred when I had to confront the ugly reality that an African American female graduate student in my department would not be able to assist me in interviewing teachers at a local high school. Through an intermediary, the teachers made it clear that although they would be polite to her, they would not provide her with useful information because of her race. Even as a researcher, I knew I would not be able to get past my own feelings of repugnance for their attitudes, so as a result I chose not to conduct any interviews with them.

Differences between interviewer and interviewee might occasionally require you to reconsider the direction of your project, but in most cases you will be able to transcend them. Armed with the right sorts of questions, a fully functioning tape recorder, a field journal, a strong ethical sense, and a desire to connect with your interviewee, you should be able to accomplish your goals even as a fledgling field researcher. However, once you've completed that all-important first interview—or the second one, or the twelfth one—how do you gracefully end it? Just as you must prepare for the interview and maintain your awareness during it, you have to decide how to conclude it.

Terminating the Interview

With any luck, the process of ending an interview is the reverse of starting it. You turn off the tape, give your thanks, and possibly provide more details about the research. Sometimes, however, the situation becomes more complicated.

After the termination of the interview, some respondents continue to talk, about things related and unrelated to the research topic. The interviewee might be lonely or eager to please; he or she might have found the experience highly pleasurable and doesn't want it to end. An ethical question researchers face involves determining whether things said after the tape is stopped can be considered part of the interview.

If you conduct an interview in someone's home, he or she might offer at the end of the interview to show you the house or yard. Field researchers who prioritize social relationships take the tour. One graduate student told me she hung in there, looking through a photo album, drinking the worst coffee she had tasted in her life, and resisting her urge to ask for a beer. Often, however, we do not have the luxury of time to remain long after the interview. As with many aspects of the interview process, be prepared: Have a courteous strategy planned for declining requests to stay longer.

You are now familiar with two different techniques for data collection: observations and interviews. In the next chapter, I present field notes as another way of creating data, as well as recording data from observations, interactions, and interviews.

Chapter Highlights

1. Interviews can be unstructured, semistructured, or structured.

2. Informal interviews resemble conversations with little standardization of format or questions.

3. Informal interviews are reciprocal, with both the researcher and the participants engaging in dialogue.

4. Interviews do not always result in useful data and willing participants.

5. Structured interviews have predetermined questions and an interview guide that is closely followed.

6. Semistructured interviews incorporate some predetermined questions while still allowing for considerable flexibility.

7. Good interview questions often start with "how" and "what."

8. Asking probes and follow-up questions is important for gaining additional information during interviews.

9. Interviewers should make sure that they ask questions relevant for addressing their research questions.

10. Establishing rapport and tending to the relationship aspect of interviews can increase their quality.

11. Status characteristics and ethical concerns are ever-present during interviews.

Exercises

1.   Select a topic of interest to you. Prepare an interview guide and conduct a structured interview with a friend. Then hold an informal interview on the same topic with another friend. Compare the procedures and your results.

2.   Using a search engine such as Google, search for the words *rapport inter-view*. Summarize what you find about establishing rapport in a job interview. Compare establishing rapport in job interviews with establishing rapport when interviewing in fieldwork. In what ways is rapport in the two venues similar and different?

3.   Find five academic journal articles that used interviewing as a method of data collection. In a few sentences, summarize each article. Note for each article whether the interviews were unstructured, structured, or semistructured. Make a list of the questions asked. What was the most common first word in the questions? For example, how many questions started with the word *how*?

8

Field Notes and Leaving the Field

Have you ever kept a diary? Or have you ever been required to write reading reflections in a journal for a class? If you haven't written regularly in a diary or journal, can you guess whether you would enjoy such an activity? Now, imagine being told that you have to write in a journal every day for the next year and that each entry must be teeming with detailed descriptions, paraphrased quotations, self-reflections, and profound thoughts. And, you need to type what you have written every night and keep your entries organized for easy retrieval. Welcome to field notes.

I can easily summarize my view of the importance of field notes to field research: If you are not writing field notes, then you are not conducting field research. Field notes serve as the repository for the important and even not-so-important data of field research. In addition, in the very act of writing them you also create data. Field note entries help us decide what we want to study. Methodological decisions are made when writing field notes, and they help maintain a certain amount of emotional stability. They assist us in our analysis, and inevitably pieces of them will find their way into the final manuscript. In a sense, field notes have a "Jack of all trades" connotation: They are at once one thing and everything.

Early in the research process, writing field notes often leads to frustration. It might help you feel more comfortable as you undertake a research project if you understand that not knowing whether you are taking field notes "right" is a common worry. Arguably, the better the field notes, the better the final product. Do not, however, let this knowledge stymie your note-taking efforts. Your notes will improve as you continue to keep them, because it is through writing that you discover important things to say. Trust the process and just keep writing.

A credit card company popularized the phrase "don't leave home without it," but it applies to your field journal—any small tablet, notebook, or maybe something aesthetically pleasing in which you write notes. The journal should be your constant companion during all stages of your research. I recommend that you choose a journal that is spiral bound or that folds flat so that you don't have to hold it open with one hand as you frantically jot notes with the other.

Now that you have your journal, how do you wield it? Again, there is no single pat answer. Although you do not have to hide taking notes during overt research, making a big production of it can be disconcerting to the participants. In order to maintain the natural flow of the interaction or interview and keep participants at ease, it is usually best if you scribble them quickly and then add more details at inconspicuous moments. Sometimes, however, members will expect that you take notes assiduously during your conversation; otherwise they might think you are not really interested in what they are saying. How do you know when to write notes and when to keep mental ones? As often happens with field situations, you will have to determine each case on the spot.

You have probably had some experiences with making these kinds of decisions. When in class, you probably are comfortable writing down as much as you can while your instructor is talking. Lofland and Lofland (1984) refer to this type of note taking as *fuller jottings* that eventually turn into full field notes when they are rewritten into more detailed form. If you visit your instructor during office hours, you might be less sure of the level of note-taking that is appropriate. If you try to remember what is being said without writing things down, Lofland and Lofland refer to this as making *mental notes*. As you know, keeping mental notes does not result in the level of detail that can be obtained from having written notes. The need for "to-do" lists is an indication that many of us find our "mental notes" insufficient. If you try to jot down some of the keywords or important points made by your instructor, in the parlance of Lofland and Lofland, you are making *jotted notes*. A problem with jotted notes is that if they are not quickly elaborated into fuller notes, their usefulness diminishes. Think about the case when you copy down bulleted points from a PowerPoint presentation. Your notes might read: (a) mutually exclusive, (b) exhaustive, and (c) theoretically meaningful. Although you have perfectly copied the items from the slide, you may not remember three weeks later what these descriptions mean or why they are important. The same advice applies to jotted notes. Although useful, jotted notes, mental notes, and fuller jottings are most useful when they are turned into full field notes, as I will describe below.

Sometimes students fail to bring something suitable for writing when they visit me during office hours. It might not matter if I don't say something worth remembering, but if I do, the student has to improvise. This happens during fieldwork too. You find yourself in the middle of something that seems important, and you are without your trusty journal. In lieu of a journal, napkins, matchbook covers, and sales receipts will do. I have even written notes on the back of my hand rather than risk forgetting. Although handy, these "in a pinch" devices are easily lost, so try to ensure that you are always prepared, journal in hand.

Content of Field Notes

Given the importance of field notes, this section of the chapter relies heavily on the work of Lofland and Lofland (1984), as it provides excellent instructions for keeping thorough and effective entries. The interested reader is encouraged to turn to the original sources for more details about field notes and field research in general. Lofland (1971) lists six types of material that typically appear in field notes.

Detailed Descriptions

The first type of information contained in field notes is *detailed descriptions* of observations and interactions in the field. Often, the descriptions are kept as a *chronological log,* with exact or approximate times of observations routinely included (Lofland & Lofland, 1984).

Such running descriptions should be concrete, replete with tangible details. Focus, as best you can, on what Lofland (1971) calls the "raw behavior"; do not attempt, at this point, to explain why someone did something or to guess how they felt when they were engaging in a particular activity. For example, if Eve told you that Nic bought her a new pottery kiln because he was happy with their relationship, make sure you write down that this is Eve's interpretation of Nic's behavior—not necessarily yours or Nic's. Later you can add your interpretation of events or other related thoughts, but when you write your initial notes, you should take extreme care to make clear distinctions among what you saw, what you think, and what people in the setting tell you (Lofland, 1971).

Detailed accounts of conversations and informal interviews that occur should be included in your notes. You should develop a system by which you can differentiate in your notes among verbatim quotes, close paraphrases, and general recall. You might put double quotation marks around verbatim material, single quotation marks around paraphrasing, and no quotation marks when you think you have captured the gist of someone's statement but are not using his or her words. Although what people say is not always what they mean, is not necessarily consistent with their behaviors, and is misinterpreted when taken out of context, the words of the members in the setting still play a large part in helping us understand the setting.

In a useful document, *Case Study Evaluations* (General Accounting Office, 1990), for individuals wishing to learn more about case studies, the General Accounting Office provides examples of two sets of notes based on an interview with a director of a small grant program who was asked how the program informed colleges about the grants. The first example is referred to as a *thin note* because it lacks detail: "The current system is to mail copies of the announcements to the chairs of relevant science departments, such as chemistry, biology, physics, and computer science" (p. 53).

Their second example based on the same interview is a *rich note* because of the amount of detail:

> The Director indicated that procedures had changed three times since the inception of the program. In the first 4 years, announcements were mailed to the individual named as president in the listing, for the same year, of the American Association of Small Colleges. Because applications were very sparse, with about 30% of eligible colleges applying, the procedure was changed to a two-stage mailing, first to the president to find out the name of the official in charge of federal programs and then to the official. This worked well for a 5-year period, in terms of receipt of applications from over 80% of the eligible colleges, but when overall federal funding for research was reduced, the positions of federal program coordinators were abolished and applications fell to about 40% of eligible institutions responding. Two years ago, the decision was made to mail copies to the persons listed as chairs of the relevant science college in appropriate professional association listings. This has increased the cost of outreach by about $15,000 or about 25% more than the prior system. To date, returns are at the 80% rate again. (General Accounting Office, 1990, p. 53)

Practice can help develop skills required for taking the kind of notes exemplified in this second example. I suspect that notes with this kind of detail probably started as jotted notes—key words and numerical information written down as memory cues. Then as quickly as possible, the jotted notes were probably translated into fuller jotted notes; this might have been done immediately after the interview while sitting in a lobby or parked car, for example. While expanding the keywords into larger segments and sentences, the researcher then will recall and add other details from the interview. Some researchers keep tape recorders in their cars so that they can record additional memories from the interview. Upon arriving home, they immediately—while the experience is still fresh—expand all notes and memories into full field notes.

Many field researchers supplement the running description with visual aids, such as maps, diagrams, and photographs. Often, they collect objects—programs, newspaper articles, menus, and brochures that can be included with the field notes.

Things Previously Forgotten

A second category of material in the field notes includes *things previously forgotten* and now remembered (Lofland, 1971). Sometimes, days later, something is recalled from an interview or observation. For example, you might finally remember what a key word from a jotted note meant. Occasionally, a behavior is recalled that had previously seemed insignificant and now seems worthy of note, possibly because a similar behavior appeared again. Such recollections get integrated into the field notes on the day they are recalled, with the time, date, and context of the original experience included—or they also can be added to the notes from the day the event occurred. In cases of an interview, I usually return to the notes from the interview and insert there what I have remembered. In that way, all relevant material for a single experience is kept in a single location.

Analytic Ideas and Inferences

The third type of material in the field notes consists of the *analytic ideas and inferences* that you will begin to have (Lofland, 1971). You might have some ideas about the social meanings of particular events or notice patterns that seem to fit a conceptual category. Write down your interpretations of interactions. Are you noticing patterns that are worth exploring? If so, write them down. What are possible theoretical implications of the interactions? Think routinely about the goals of your study and write down any potential insights you have about them. Ideas that seem trivial, obvious, and far-fetched are all acceptable. Put all ideas—good, bad, and those about which you're uncertain—in the field notes. This process of creating complete field notes constitutes part of your analysis. The more analysis that occurs in conjunction with the creation of field notes, the easier the project will be to complete (Lofland, 1971).

Personal Feelings

The fourth type of material in the field notes involves your *personal feelings* (Lofland, 1971). If in the setting you were scared, happy, bored, or frustrated, write it down. What person did you like—and what person did you not? Did you think an interaction went well or did you feel completely stupid? Although feelings and impressions might not seem relevant to our carefully constructed and scientific research project, they are, in fact, often a rich source of analytic insights. Personal feelings have their roots in social events. If you are feeling a certain way, others might be too, so this feeling might be a worthy avenue to explore. Also, your emotional reactions to people and events affect them and shape your interpretation of them. If you keep a record of your emotions, you will find yourself in a better position to analyze the dynamics of your interactions (Lofland & Lofland, 1984).

Things to Think About and Do

The fifth element in field notes is *things to think about and do* (Lofland, 1971). If you need to go back and collect a missing detail, write it down. If you have ideas that you want to follow up on, write these down (Lofland & Lofland, 1984). What questions might be good to ask? Did you fail to talk to someone today who you would like to see tomorrow? Before each observational period, review your "to do" list from the previous day. Forward items not completed onto the next day's notes.

Reflexive Thoughts

The sixth type of material contained in field notes is your *reflexive thoughts*. This category overlaps with the others, particularly personal feelings. The role of **reflexivity** has become so important since the 1960s that there was said to be a "reflexive turn" in qualitative research (Altheide & Johnson, 1994, p. 485).

Although varied and complicated definitions of reflexivity exist, I define the concept as the researcher's active consideration of his or her place in the research. Although field research is not singularly about you as the researcher, you are "part and parcel of the setting, context, and culture" (Altheide & Johnson, 1994, p. 486) you are trying to understand. You are the instrument of data collection; you analyze and interpret the data; you write the final product. Whether during your project you take an objective stance and write in a passive voice in the third person, express your values and write in an active voice in the first person, or create a poem from your experiences, you are always unavoidably present and necessary in field research. Field notes provide you with an excellent location in which to struggle with how you and your decisions are embedded in the research. What you learn from the experience of reflexive writing can become incorporated into the final manuscript, giving readers additional details for evaluating your research.

Early in his book about residents of East Harlem, Bourgois (1995) wrote that in his case "self-conscious reflexivity was especially necessary and useful" because he was "an outsider from the larger society's dominant class, ethnicity, and gender categories who was attempting to study the experience of inner-city poverty among Puerto Ricans" (p. 13). His goal was to convey the "individual experience of social structural oppression," including racial segregation and economic marginalization; yet, to do so—analytically, theoretically, and ethically—he would have to include "even the goriest details" of the lives of people he had befriended, details that he knew could be used to justify further oppression (pp. 15–18). Bourgois shares with his readers the struggles he underwent as he attempted to decide what information to include from thousands of pages of recorded conversations. In one instance, for example, he had to determine whether to include the details of a conversation between two men about a rape. He shares his reflections about how the rape had shaken some of the social relationships formed during his fieldwork:

> Despite the almost three years that I had already spent on the street at the time of this particular conversation, I was unprepared to face this dimension of gendered brutality. I kept asking myself how it was possible that I had invested so much energy into taking these 'psychopaths'

seriously. On a more personal level, I was confused because the rapists had already become my friends. With notable individual exceptions, I had grown to like most of these veteran rapists. I was living with the enemy; it had become my social network. They had engulfed me in the common sense of street culture until their rape accounts forced me to draw the line. (p. 207)

Although what you have just read is the polished version of Bourgois's reflections, the seeds of the final version may have been contained in his field notes.

Guidelines for Writing Field Notes

At this point, specific guidelines for taking notes in the field might be help-ful. If you are a beginning researcher, I suggest that you limit your interac-tions and observations to three-hour blocks. It is difficult to pay close attention for much longer than that, and at any one time we can retain only a limited amount of information. Second, write your field notes as soon as possible after each observational period. The more time that elapses, the less you will remember. If you conduct an interview with a member in the morning, try to write your field notes in the afternoon. However, if you conduct your observations in the evening, you usually can wait until early the next morning to record your notes, as during sleep you retain fairly detailed memory (Lofland & Lofland, 1984). The worst situation for reten-tion occurs when you attempt to create field notes for two observational periods or interviews simultaneously. You may forget many of the events and the analytic insights you experienced during the first encounter, and you will remember far less from the second than you might imagine.

The number of pages of field notes generated per observational period varies greatly. Lofland and Lofland (1984, p. 67) suggest that approximately 13 pages of field notes should result from each hour's observation! It will take you at least as long to write your field notes as it took to observe—in most cases, probably twice as long. Some researchers find that they spend three to four hours typing field notes for every hour of field observations.

Although you should always have a field journal with you to record on-the-spot notes, remember that the data contained in it should be typed, each night if possible. Even if you conduct formal interviews that you will transcribe, the notes in the field journal should be typed.

Otherwise, you might end up focusing your analysis on the interviews and giving short shrift to the journal notes, in which some of your keenest insights might be recorded.

Find a way to keep your notes organized, and if you make any changes or move material, make sure you create a formal log to explain what you have done. Do not trust your memory. Keep one copy as a master that is never touched. Cut, paste, and play with duplicates.

And need I say back up all computer files regularly? You will no doubt have multiple copies on your hard drive, but I suggest that you back up all files daily on a removable device: an external hard drive, a zip disk, a flash or thumb drive. Although the method is more expensive, you might even choose to make hard copies so that if all the technology in your home fails, you can at least have a good old-fashioned paper file with which to work. Store copies of your field notes in some other location, such as the office of an instructor or committee chair.

If you think writing field notes sounds tedious, you are right. Most of the writing and typing is not particularly fun. Occasionally, you might enjoy writing about a particular interaction in the setting, but a lot of the creation of field notes is hard work. You will be tempted to put it off, but persevere. Once you form the habit of routinely writing field notes, the task will become easier (Lofland & Lofland, 1984). Remind yourself that what is not written in the field notes that day will be lost forever.

Leaving the Field

Field research, by definition, involves long-term interactions. Whereas any project you undertake for class will probably last no more than a few days or weeks, most field research requires months or years in the field. At some point, the researcher decides that it is time to end the fieldwork portion of the research. Many factors influence the decision to leave the field. One's safety is a factor. Most researchers agree that if your safety, either physical or psychological, is at risk you should leave the field immediately. This is true whether you just arrived in a setting or have been there for months. You should also leave if the participants in the setting no longer want you there.

Practical matters can influence the decision to leave the field. Some academics can conduct fieldwork only during academic breaks that occur during summer months or during sabbaticals. Running out of money is another reason field researchers leave the field—a condition that graduate students often experience.

Sometimes field researchers know it is time to stop the fieldwork when they feel that they are not learning anything new. One way you will know when you are reaching such a saturation point is when the "things to do" portion of your field notes grows relatively small. More important, when you are drawing fewer and fewer analytic insights from active participation in the setting, you might decide to attempt closure.

Regardless of what motivated the decision to terminate the fieldwork portion of the research, concern for the relationships formed in the setting should be primary while exiting. Think about not only your needs but also those of the individuals you have met in the setting. By now, you probably have become close friends with several people. Some have come to depend upon you.

One way of caring for these relationships is to discuss and plan your leaving with the participants. Make sure that you have done all the things that you said you would. Another way of caring for these relationships is to consider whether future contact with the participants is appropriate. A frequent reason for contact with the participants after leaving the field is to allow them to respond to a draft of the completed manuscript. More will be said about **member checks** later in this guide.

The analysis of your data starts when you first consider engaging in field research and continues long after you have left the field. In the next chapter, you will begin your exploration of various techniques used for analyzing data.

Chapter Highlights

1. Field notes are the backbone of collecting and analyzing field data.

2. Field notes consist of mental notes, jotted notes, fuller notes, and the full field notes themselves.

3. Field notes contain detailed descriptions of events, things previously forgotten, analytic ideas and inferences, impressions and personal feelings, things to think about and do, and reflexive thoughts.

4. Field notes should be completed soon after each observational period, and they may take twice as long to write as the time spent observing.

5. Ending the fieldwork portion of one's research requires attention to relationships created in the setting.

Exercises

1.   Go to a setting where you have never been before. Observe this setting for 10 minutes without taking any notes. Wait 24 hours then type a detailed account of as many things as you can remember. A day later, go to another setting where you have never been before. Observe this setting for 10 minutes taking detailed notes about your observations. Wait 24 hours and then write as many things as you can remember about this second setting using your notes. Compare your two descriptions. What did you learn from this exercise? Do you think the results of this exercise would be the same if the two observation periods were three hours long?

2.   Keep a running log, or field notes, throughout the day of your feelings and emotional reactions to events. Using the notes, write a detailed summary of your emotional state during the day. Then write an equally detailed description about the process of taking these kinds of notes. For example, did you carry a journal specifically for this exercise, or did you jot notes with your class notes? Did your notes include times and details about the situations that triggered your emotions? Were you able to remember to jot notes about yourself on a regular basis?

3.   Allan Roadburg writes that the form of interaction between the researcher and participants is unique insofar as neither party has any control over the fact that the termination of the relationship coincides with the termination of the research. If individuals wish to continue a relationship after the research has concluded, it will no longer be a researcher–participant relationship but will be based on different criteria (1980, p. 281). Do you agree with these statements? Justify your answer. What are the implications of them for the field research process?

9

Coding, Memoing, and Descriptions

After prolonged interactions in the field, researchers focus their attention on the difficult process of analyzing the myriad information collected there. The multipronged process of **analysis** requires that the researcher make sense of the data: break it down, study its components, investigate its importance, and interpret its meanings. Despite the inherent value of analysis to field research, however, few concrete and easily understood instructions exist regarding how to gain analytical insight into the data one has collected. Indeed, some suggest that data analysis is more of an art than a technique. Even if that is the case, artists benefit from training. Thus, in this chapter I offer some general advice to the beginning field researcher, as well as a menu of options used by seasoned professionals. I begin this survey of analytical techniques with a discussion of coding, memoing, and descriptions.

Although we tend to think of analysis as a process that starts after all the data has been collected, it actually begins at the moment the researcher starts to think about conducting a field research project. It continues during each stage of the research process, such as gaining entrée, building relationships, observing and interacting in the field, interviewing, and writing field notes. Finally, analysis helps structure the production of the final manuscript. Although analysis is ongoing, one completes a considerable portion of it after one has left the field.

Usually, the researcher can expect to devote a greater amount of time to analysis than what was spent in the field; in fact, Lofland and Lofland (1984) estimate the time one spends analyzing to be two to five times more than one spends collecting data. Consequently, if you are interested in field research because you believe it will be faster and easier to complete than more quantitative forms of analysis, you will find this not to be the case.

Some of the procedures for analyzing qualitative data parallel those used for quantitative data, with which you might be more familiar. At first just a "bunch of numbers," quantitative data becomes meaningful only after researchers use specific techniques to compile and organize it. First, the raw data are entered into a software program such as **SPSS**. Then researchers must know which statistical tests and procedures are most appropriate for testing their hypotheses; cross-tabulations, *t*-tests, analysis of variance, multiple regression, and logit are just a few of the many options. After finishing their initial analysis, researchers then make conclusions about the substantive and statistical significance of the data.

Like their quantitative counterparts, qualitative researchers also gather data. At first, the data are just a "bunch of words" that, like numbers, reveal meaning only after being compiled and organized. On the basis of their research questions, qualitative researchers determine and apply the analytical strategies that best serve their purpose. Only then can they interpret the results of their analysis. Regardless of these general similarities, however, the process of actually analyzing data arguably becomes more difficult for the qualitative researcher. Indeed, things can get quite ugly.

When approaching hundreds of pages of text to be analyzed, it is easy to feel overwhelmed. One student reported to me that her head contained so many different options for analyzing her data that she feared its weight would make her topple over. Her fear never became a reality, of course, but she nonetheless felt the stress of the decisions with which she was faced. Eventually, she settled on three techniques for analyzing her data and completed an impressive dissertation

To help you avoid a fear of toppling, I present only 10 of the many options you have for analyzing your data. Because almost all analytical techniques feature **coding** and **memoing**, I begin with them. After a brief review of software programs that aid the coding process, I present the topic of descriptions as an analytical technique. Chapter 10 will consider typologies, taxonomies, visual representations, and themes, followed in Chapter 11 with storytelling, critical events, and analytical induction. Because many excellent sources exist on how to analyze quantitative data that is sometimes generated during fieldwork, I do not review those procedures in this guide.

In addition to experiencing difficulty applying a particular technique, several other factors complicate the analytical process. First, the analytical techniques presented here are not mutually exclusive. For example, all techniques—not merely one or even two—include an element of description. Second, the differences among them often are subtle which makes choosing the most appropriate technique more difficult. Third, sometimes more than a single technique is appropriate, even required. Because using one method instead of another significantly affects what eventually gets reported to the reader, decisions are not made lightly. Fourth, techniques for analyzing data are interwoven in complicated patterns with styles of presentation in the final manuscript, a concern you will understand more clearly once you have read about the different techniques.

Massive amounts of data are generated during fieldwork. For example, Bourgois (1995) reported that he edited thousands of pages of transcriptions. Nonetheless, an essential component of data analysis requires that you become so familiar with the data that it feels like a friend—admittedly one who you don't always like. There is simply no escaping repeated reading of and interacting with your data. One of the ways that researchers interact is through **coding**.

Coding

Coding is the process of organizing a large amount of data into smaller segments that, when needed, can be retrieved easily. When I think about coding, I am reminded of the quote attributed to Martin Fischer, "Knowledge is a process of piling up facts: wisdom lies in their simplification" (ThinkExist.com, 2005). Data reduction, simplification, lies at the heart of coding.

Note that I did not define coding as the process of finding "themes that emerge from the data." Although field researchers commonly use this phrase, I avoid it because I believe that equating coding with thematic analysis obscures the many other approaches to qualitative analysis. Further, and probably more important, I do not believe that insights "emerge" from the data. One does not search through one's qualitative garden at the right time of year and find themes like daffodils emerging from the ground. Qualitative researchers actively create the final product that they believe adequately represents their observations and interactions. The initial idea, the research questions, data collection, coding, interpretation, and writing of the final manuscript are all functions of the researchers' decisions and actions. Thus, themes do not wait in the data to emerge so that we all can see them. Obviously, the setting and members limit the parameters of raw materials from which the researcher works, but the researcher controls what is produced from these ingredients.

Making the data manageable is a daunting task. To describe the process, I use the metaphor of being inside a fabric store, armed only with the instructions that I have to *make something*. I have free access to all sorts of materials, patterns, crafts, buttons, sewing machines, scissors, and trims, but these items are piled together haphazardly in the center of the store. Even worse, I have only a vague idea of how to sew. One thing is certain, though: I know that organizing all the materials in the store will make things easier for me when I have to make decisions regarding what I will make. Thus, I begin by labeling all the items, knowing that I will soon put those with the same label into the same pile. For example, I identify all the fabrics and then put them together in a corner. Sometimes I am not sure what label something should get—is a button just a button or is it also a trim?—so I assign it more than one label. A few items I label as miscellaneous or just leave in the original pile. I might also create a list of things that I thought should be in the store but that are missing. If I can find no thread, for example, I would make a note about this so I could follow up on why it isn't there.

Initial Coding

What this metaphor describes is the process of **initial coding**, sometimes called **open coding** (Strauss & Corbin, 1990). As field researchers, we engage in this process in order to break up multiple pages of text into more manageable segments that can be grouped together and used during later stages of the analysis (Hesse-Biber & Leavy, 2006).

During initial coding, researchers repeatedly read their data and code as much of it as possible. Warren and Karner (2005) provide an example of 16 responses made by one respondent to an interviewer's questions. Twenty different codes were attached to these responses. For example, the statement "Well I don't know how to explain it but, many men that's been to VN, man, I don't need that stuff" has two codes: "Contradiction between account and behavior of talking" and "Cultural products for those who weren't there" (p. 192). You might be relieved to know that Warren and Karner are skilled researchers who know their topic well, so they can code at a higher conceptual level than is expected of most beginning researchers. Not every bit of data from months of observations, interactions, interviews, and writing field notes will be coded. However, you should read every line of data, code whatever you think might be potentially useful for analysis, knowing that later, more codes will be added, some changed, and large sections of coded data will go unused.

To return to my fabric store metaphor, I now have reached the point where I have organized the items into groups of similar objects, but I still have far too many piles to be able to use them effectively. I know it will help if I organize similar groups of items into a larger category that subsumes them. For example, I realize that items I labeled zippers, snaps, and buttons could be categorized together under the classification "closures." Having all items together that simplify the task of putting on and taking off the item of clothing I am likely to make will facilitate my decision when I am ready to select what I will use for this purpose. At this stage, I also start to pick out items that I might potentially use; I identify a few fabrics that I like, then I find buttons and thread to match.

Focused Coding

At this stage in my metaphorical fabric store, I am engaging in **focused coding**, sometimes referred to as **axial coding** (Strauss & Corbin, 1990). When you undertake focused coding, you further reduce the data by identifying and combining the initial coded data into larger categories that subsume multiple codes. For example, items that might have been labeled during initial coding as "doing things with father" and "mother scolding" could be put together into a category called "family interactions." Your goal in focused coding involves moving from a fairly literal code (zipper) into a more conceptual one (closure items) (Hesse-Biber & Leavy, 2006). Focused coding also involves hunting for specific targets. For example, a researcher might take a pass through the data looking only for instances of gendered interactions.

How does the two-stage process of coding work when applied to actual fieldwork? For her dissertation, Sharon McGuire (1998) engaged in a complex coding strategy. She wanted to understand at-risk, first-year college students' perceptions of their academic performance activities. These students were enrolled in a structured academic intervention program (p. 28). During her open coding stage, McGuire coded all the student comments and behaviors that related to their performance activities, such as "working at the library" and "talking about a faculty member as a mentor."

Subsequently, during focused coding, McGuire (1998) organized the relevant codes into four larger dimensions: "studying activities," "interactions with faculty," "perceptions of grades," and "mental engagement in academic work." She then recoded her data again to identify variations within each of the larger dimensions. For example, for "studying activities," she created categories such as "expectations for studying," "perceptions of the need to study," and "preferred style of studying." Then, she recoded the data yet again, looking for subtypes of these categories. "Clear expectations" and "unclear expectations" were two subcategories for "expectations for studying." Figure 9.1 presents a partial representation of her coding outcomes. Note that for all categories, McGuire would have made sure that she could easily retrieve the data from which they were created.

Strategies for Improving Coding

Like Emeril Lagasse, a master chef and television personality, who "kicks" his dishes "up a notch" by adding additional garlic or other seasonings, the goal of moving from open to focused coding involves kicking the raw materials in the field notes and transcriptions up to a level that facilitates your ability to make analytical insights into the setting. This level might involve connections to previous research on the topic, concerns of the researcher's discipline, or theoretical concepts (Warren & Karner, 2005). Ideally, one can attach to concrete experiences and words such conceptual codes as social marginalization and alienation (Bourgois, 1995), informal social control (Duneier, 1999), knowledge evolution (Garrahy, Kulinna, & Cothran, 2005), development and continuity of subcultures (Prus & Irini, 1988), and identity politics (Stein, 2001).

As should be clear by now, you can create useful insights into the setting more easily when you are well grounded in your discipline; if you want to conduct a sociological, anthropological, or educational analysis of a setting, you will be well served if you are well versed in sociology, anthropology, or educational research. The researcher is like the magician trying to pull the rabbit out of the hat; the more training the magician has had, the more likely the rabbit will appear.

Certainly, you should begin this process of immersion in your discipline by reading the academic literature on your topic. By reading previous research, you can become familiar with what others have learned about a setting similar to yours. This will help you think about how previous researchers' findings compare with your data and analysis.

Although you should become well grounded in the literature, take care not to feel constrained by what others have found; rather, use their

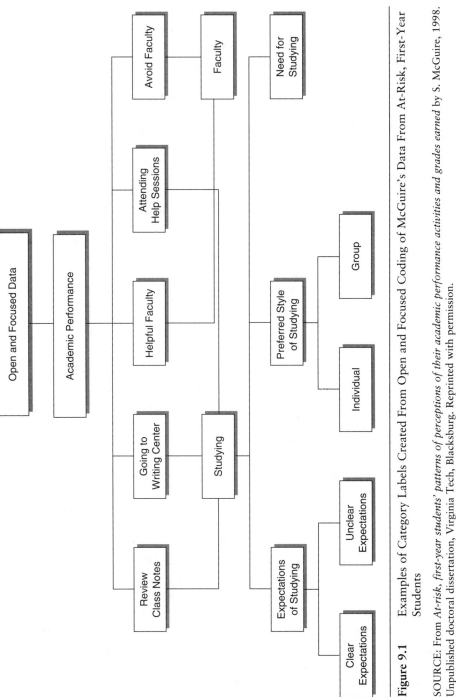

Figure 9.1 Examples of Category Labels Created From Open and Focused Coding of McGuire's Data From At-Risk, First-Year Students

SOURCE: From *At-risk, first-year students' patterns of perceptions of their academic performance activities and grades earned* by S. McGuire, 1998. Unpublished doctoral dissertation, Virginia Tech, Blacksburg. Reprinted with permission.

insights as launching pads for your own (Jorgensen, 1989). For example, in preparing her dissertation, McGuire (1998) had to free herself from the literature before she felt like she was making progress analyzing her data from at-risk college students. She wrote,

> My coding was going along methodically when I began to explore my own experiences in relation to what I was coding. I read Krieger's (1985) insightful piece on coming to terms with yourself in relation to your data. I realized that what I knew of the perceptions of at-risk, first-year students was shaped by my experiences I have had as a student, a student affairs professional and as a teacher. My analytical perspective was solely based on the literature. I had not myself experienced academic difficulty in high school or college. Also, unlike the students whose stories I was analyzing, I am a third generation college student who grew up in a white suburban middle-class neighborhood in northern California. This acknowledgement was very freeing because it allowed me to set aside what the literature was telling me and really listen to the words of my students. I had gotten "stuck" in my analysis because my lens through which to explore the data did not illuminate the students' perceptions and experiences. In other words, the literature did not seem to fit the majority of the stories I was reading. (p. 29)

Notice how McGuire seamlessly includes reflexive statements about how her status characteristics and familiarity with the literature affected her analysis. I have included the example from McGuire (1998), in part, because of the level of detail she provides in the methods section about her coding process. Coding, as with other features of one's methodology, is not ignored in the final manuscript. Providing detailed explanations of one's coding procedures is one of many ways that researchers improve the trustworthiness, a concept discussed in the last chapter, of their research.

Another suggestion for improving your analysis involves talking about your research, a topic that I will explore in depth in the final chapter of this guide. Talk to your instructor, the chair of your thesis committee, your best friend, your partner, other researchers, or your parents. Brainstorm, wax philosophical, extend scenarios to weird extremes, posit structural explanations, and talk to anyone who is a good conversationalist and willing to listen. Talking, like writing, can be a way of clarifying thoughts and gaining insights. To illustrate, McGuire (1998) notes in her methods section that in an effort to help her identify core concepts from her data, she talked to her graduate assistant and peer instructor. Obviously, you should take care not to violate the confidentiality of anyone in the setting when you talk about your research with others.

Clearly, initial coding and focused coding play important roles in analysis, but some disagreement exists as to whether they are, in and of themselves, analytical. Some scholars view coding as a mechanical process that informs the analysis but is not analysis per se. In contrast, I agree with Miles and Huberman (1994) who assert "[c]oding is analysis" (p. 56). Field researchers have research questions and conceptual frames that provide valuable guidance for coding things in a way that, hopefully, will be useful when they create the final manuscript. Since the researcher must make decisions about what to code and how to code it, I believe this process serves as an important element of the analysis. In spite of its importance, coding is far from a sufficient activity for analysis.

Memoing

In conjunction with coding, field researchers simultaneously engage in the process of **memoing,** essentially the writing of memos to oneself regarding insights one derives from coding and reflecting on the data. During this memoing stage, the researcher creates, defines, and refines conceptual categories, makes tentative notes about links between concepts, and draws a sketch—often literally as well as metaphorically—of features important for understanding the setting.

Coding and memoing are iterative processes. For example, during initial coding, I attached the code "silenced; council ignores testimony" to a section of an interview where a woman said that she was frustrated when county supervisors ignored what she had to say when she attended their meetings. In the focused coding stage, I revisited the initial code and added "lack of political efficacy" as a code. During memoing, I attempted to define political efficacy using various sections of the interviews to refine my conceptual definition.

When I yet again returned to the sections of the interviews with political efficacy codes, I noticed that I had also labeled "lack of social networks" in nearby sections of the interviews. In a memo to myself, I wrote about the possibility of social networks being a vehicle for enhancing political efficacy. I included verbatim text from the interviews to support my hypothesis that social networks and political efficacy might be related. Since my focused coding also suggested a link between political efficacy and social class, I also made notes to myself to review the literature on these two concepts. Now that I had a better idea regarding the concept of political efficacy and its relationships with other concepts, I used **selective coding** on my interview transcripts. This time, I attempted to code the data at an even higher conceptual level.

Memoing, like most of the procedures used during analysis, requires asking questions, posing hypotheses, and seeking answers grounded in the data. In addition, memos are data for subsequent analysis. Sometimes field researchers use computer software to help them with the coding and memoing process.

Computer-Assisted Qualitative Data Analysis

Computers have become standard equipment for field researchers. The list created by Miles and Huberman (1994) more than a decade ago still presents a good summary of the ways that researchers use computers:

1. Making notes in the field

2. Writing up or transcribing field notes

3. Editing: correcting, extending or revising field notes

4. Coding: attaching key words or tags to segments of text to permit later retrieval

5. Storage: keeping text in an organized database

6. Search and retrieval: locating relevant segments of text and making them available for inspection

7. Data "linking": connecting relevant data segments with each other, forming categories, clusters or networks of information

8. Memoing: writing reflective commentaries on some aspect of data, as a basis for deeper understanding

9. Content analysis: counting frequencies, sequence or locations of words and phrases

10. Data display: Placing selected or reduced data in a condensed organized format, such as a matrix or network, for inspection

11. Conclusion drawing and verification: aiding the analyst to interpret displayed data and to test or confirm findings

12. Theory building: developing systematic, conceptually coherent explanations of findings; testing hypotheses

13. Graphic mapping: creating diagrams that depict findings or theories

14. Preparing interim and final reports. (p. 44)

I include this list because it serves as a review and foreshadows some of the techniques discussed later in this chapter.

Although many researchers consider computers essential tools and often use specialized software programs for data analysis, others prefer more traditional methods. Some researchers elect to print, cut, and paste hard copies of their data and code it with colored pencils, and others use applications not specifically designed for qualitative data, such as Microsoft Word. One graduate student I worked with used an elaborate array of colored post-it notes. However, the use of specialized software for qualitative data analysis is becoming increasingly common, perhaps because newer generations of such programs boast smaller learning curves and more capabilities than did earlier versions.

Once you have decided to use computer-assisted qualitative data analysis software, you will have to determine which software program will be most helpful. Ideally, selecting this program should be a "principled choice . . . that matches the capabilities of the software to the specific needs of the researcher and the project" (Weitzman, 1999, p. 1241). Realistically, however, your choice often will be guided by other factors, such as cost, personal preferences, computer platform, recommendations by others, and level of training required for proficiency.

Newer generations of software programs allow for coding, memoing, finding keywords in context, and retrieving segments of data. Since they allow the researcher to explore links that specify relationships among codes, create higher order categories, organize conceptual categories hierarchically, and test theoretical propositions, they are particularly useful to the process of theory building. Some of these programs can assist in making graphic representations of relationships among concepts (Weitzman, 1999).

Among the wide variety of choices now available to researchers are ATLAS.ti, HyperRESEARCH, MAXqda2, Nvivo, N6, CDC EZ-text, Qualrus, QDA Miner, and Ethnograph (Lewins & Silver, 2005). A larger list, developer links, estimated prices, and comparisons of different programs easily can be found online.

Although computer-assisted qualitative data analysis programs are particularly useful for large field research projects, smaller ones can be completed successfully without the use of such sophisticated technologies. If you are a beginner, I recommend that you analyze your data without computer-aided technology: By doing so, you will learn more about the actual nuts and bolts of the analytical process, and the experience might lead to more effective use of software for future projects.

Regardless of all the useful tools these software programs provide, they cannot actually perform an analysis. I believe that having the right tool for the job can certainly make all sorts of tasks easier; however, in order to be an effective practitioner of his or her craft, the builder, repairer, or researcher must know how to use the tools, have a plan for using them, and use them appropriately. On the basis of this strongly held belief in the value of learning "by hand," I devote the remaining space in this chapter to other analytical techniques commonly employed by researchers without further discussion of software. I begin with descriptions.

Descriptions

A fairly uncontested and extremely important aspect of field research manuscripts involves detailed descriptions of the setting, interactions, and observations that have occurred over a prolonged period of time. Because other analytical techniques discussed here involve description, and because, in my opinion, a large portion of the final manuscript should be descriptive in nature, I devote more space to descriptions than to some other approaches discussed in this guide.

The purpose of descriptions is to answer what are typically referred to as the "reporter's questions": *Who? What? Why? Where? When?* and *How? What is going on in the setting? Which actors were present? What did the place or setting look like? What did the researcher see, and what was reported to the researcher by others* (Wolcott, 1994, p. 12)?

Although generous portions of descriptions are included in final manuscripts, readers will not need or even want to know everything. As Wolcott (1994) said, "I don't want the 'raw' data, I want it 'cooked'" (p. 13). Readers will not need to know about every object in the room— *the pencil was a standard #2, yellow in color and with an eraser on one end*—nor will they need to know every action undertaken by participants—*Susan scratched her hair three times in quick succession with the little finger of her left hand.* As a field researcher, you will learn to select portions of what you saw and experienced and present them to the reader in a way that highlights important items and omits irrelevant ones. When you seek to understand and describe a setting, part of the analytical work involves your ability to decide what to include and how much detail to provide.

Thick Descriptions

Thick descriptions (Geertz, 1973) are almost a requirement for field research—although you might not ever know with certainty what is "thick" enough and, in some cases, you can provide what is essentially a broad yet detailed overview. As noted previously, try to have descriptions in your field notes so "thick" they are like concrete. In the final manuscript, you selectively use detailed chunks that support your narrative or that make the scene easy for the reader to visualize.

Returning to Russell's (1991) study of homeless women, one can see how she provided thick, although brief, descriptions:

> Ada, for example, is between 55 and 65. Her head seems grotesquely misshapen on one side because of the huge mass of her grey-white hair, which she tries to cover with a scarf. Many of her teeth are missing and her face is deeply lined. Even in the warmth of a May evening she wears layers of clothes. Her legs are swollen and ulcerated, and her bare feet, propped on a box, are black with grime. (p. 1)

> Henrietta, with an ill-fitting golden brown wig sitting somewhat askew on her head, her face heavily lined for a woman just turned 51, sits in the day shelter and tries to hide the fact that she has no upper teeth. She says, "I'm fifty-one already. I didn't realize it. I didn't get any cards or anything." (p. 2)

These descriptions provide strong visual images for the reader, particularly because in Western culture one's hair is often a clue about the self. A "thinner" description, such as "one woman had grey-white hair, and another woman who is 51 wore a golden brown wig," falls flat in comparison. Knowing that Ada wore layers of clothes during the warmth of May also is an important detail. However, if Russell had described the color of Ada's outer layer of clothes, then the next, and the next, I'm not sure she would have provided readers with any added value from these details. Yet, if Ada's coat, sweater, shirt, skirt, and shoes were all in the same shade of red, then that detail might be worth giving the reader.

Research Questions

Descriptions that provide insights into your research questions are particularly helpful. At times, it is useful to explicitly convey why you include some information (Wolcott, 1994, p. 14). If you find that you have difficulty articulating your reasons for including particular details, then maybe you should omit that portion of the description—or dig deeper to determine its value. For example, Chenault (2004) once learned that a resident in the community she was studying had been seen, more than once, having sex in the laundromat. She included this detail in a draft of her dissertation. When I pressed her to tell me why she included this information, the best response she could offer is that she thought it was "pretty wild." Realizing this incident did not illuminate her research questions, she wisely deleted it from the next draft. Details that are sexy, either literally or metaphorically, do not always belong in a final manuscript.

As an illustration of how researchers use description to illuminate or underscore their key questions, Russell (1991) begins her book about homeless women with a detailed description of one woman, and then her next paragraph explicitly connects this description to a central question of her book. Russell writes,

> She sat in the corner of the large room, staring into space. Suddenly, her arms began to wave wildly and her face contorted and twisted into spasms. After 30 seconds or so, she again became still and resumed her trance-like state. I asked who she was. "She was a teacher in Baltimore City, her name is Betty, and she has recently been released from Springfield [a state mental hospital]," explained the woman in charge of the day shelter.
>
> I teach in Baltimore County, and my name is Betty Russell. In my search for who the homeless women of Baltimore are, I found the answer on the first day I visited a shelter for homeless women: the homeless can be anyone. (p. 1)

By describing the homeless women about whom she writes, Russell makes them come alive for the reader. They are not insignificant informants, but rather women who shared their lives with her, often on a daily basis. As a result, her analysis appropriately includes spending a great deal of time describing them to us. Through her descriptions, we learn of their resiliency, their will to survive, their support for each other, and many of their other positive attributes.

Summary

Descriptions are the window into the world of the setting. They should be sufficiently detailed so that the reader can "see" the participants and the setting. A good qualitative study engages the reader, and such engagement is less likely to happen if we don't "know" the participants—if we can't see, hear, even (when necessary) smell them.

Sometimes, when students are having trouble writing drafts of their manuscript, I suggest that they begin by writing a chapter devoted solely to introducing the participants in the setting. Detailed descriptions of the participants are an important feature of the final manuscript, and a chapter such as this is relatively easy and usually enjoyable to write. However, a separate chapter that introduces the members is not always warranted or even appropriate. For field research presented as a book, the authors might instead let the readers get to know the participants as their books unfolds, as was the case with Duneier (1999) and Bourgois (1995).

Detailed descriptions put the readers on the scene, helping them visualize the setting. For example, Heather Switzer (personal communication, February 22, 2005), a Ph.D. candidate, wrote the following thick and powerful description of milk she tasted during her time with the Maasai:

> Maasai milk is really more like drinkable yogurt. Startlingly white—almost shiny in the perpetually dark interior of the boma—and smooth, like white wall paint. When Maasai girls milk the cows, they collect the fresh milk in hollowed-out gourds (called a "calabash") and set them aside for a few days. The collection gourds are dried in the sun, and then the remaining seeds and inner flesh are burned away with fine embers. The gourds give the milk the distinctive smoky aroma that characterizes life in the boma. That smell—of wood smoke, fermented milk, cow urine and dung, permeates everything—air, human skin, cloth. That smell becomes the taste of the milk, and it's a tricky one to get used to.

Similar to examples presented earlier in this guide, the beauty of Switzer's description rests with her attention not only to the things she sees, but also to the things she smells. As a researcher, Switzer clearly realized that presenting one dimension of the description alone—the taste of the milk—would leave her readers with an incomplete understanding of its nature.

Although descriptions serve field researchers as an important analytical technique because they make the observed available to the reader, other techniques are equally useful. In the following chapters, I present seven other analytical techniques often used in field research.

Chapter Highlights

1. Analysis is not distinct from the other processes of conducting field research.

2. The time spent analyzing field research data is typically as long as the time it took to collect it.

3. Analyzing data requires reading and rereading one's data.

4. Coding is the process of identifying and organizing portions of the data that are potentially useful for further analyses.

5. During open coding, all data that might have any relevance for gaining insight into the setting and participants are labeled.

6. During focused coding, the researcher is attentive to particular aspects of the data.

7. Memoing is the process of writing notes or memos about thoughts related to the analysis of one's data.

8. Thick descriptions are part of almost all final manuscripts.

9. What is described should serve to provide the reader with insight into the members and the setting.

10. Part of the purpose of descriptions are to answer the questions, *who? what? why? where? when?* and *how?*

Exercises

1.   Reread this chapter and code every instance where I addressed you, the reader of this guide. How many times did I do this? Give three examples of sentences that were easy to code and three that you weren't so certain should be included. Explain your coding process—for example, did you highlight terms or write in the margins? After you identified what you thought were relevant sentences,

then what did you do? What decision rule did you use to determine what you included in your count and what you did not? How long did it take you to code the chapter?

2.   Select a public setting, such as a coffee shop, where no informed consent is required for observations. Making sure that you make no one uncomfortable, observe for 15 minutes while keeping detailed notes. Write a detailed description of the setting and individuals in it. Include information that answers the questions, *who? what? why? where? when?* and *how?*

3.   Have a friend pose for you while you take extremely detailed notes about his or her physical appearance. After the observation, write a one-page, double-spaced, physical description of your friend. The description should be a well-written narrative (not a bulleted list) and interesting to read. The description should *not* include what the person is saying or doing. However, you can include descriptions of the person's body language. The description should be only about his or her physical appearance.

10

Typologies, Taxonomies, Visual Representations, and Themes

When I think about data analysis, I am reminded of the quotation attributed to the English writer, Margery Allingham (1889–1966):

> He did not arrive at this conclusion by the decent process of quiet, logical deduction, nor yet by the blinding flash of glorious intuition, but by the shoddy, untidy process halfway between the two by which one usually gets to know things. (ThinkExist.com, 2005)

I introduce you to four more strategies for analyzing data—**typologies, taxonomies, visual representations,** and **themes**—but I know it will feel, at times, that some unnamed secret ingredient is needed to successfully analyze one's data. However, I strongly encourage you to hang in there and rigorously apply techniques you are learning in this guide or elsewhere. Hard work is more apt to make your efforts worthwhile than waiting for the muse.

Typologies

Did your high school have groups of students referred to as "stoners," "skaters," "preppies," and so on? If so, then you are already familiar with typologies. Building on systematic coding and descriptive accounts, researchers create typologies as a way of analyzing their data. At its simplest, developing typologies helps the researcher make sense of a large amount of data (high school students) by grouping them into similar categories based on common characteristics (involved in sports). The grouped data are usually given a label ("athletes") to aid in discussion of how they might be important to our understanding of a setting.

Prior to moving to a detailed presentation of typologies, a word of caution is needed. Simply putting activities, events, or individuals in boxes with snappy labels and interesting descriptions will not necessarily produce anything new, illuminating, or otherwise useful about the setting or participants. Lofland and Lofland warn us:

> We must caution you . . . that typology construction can easily become a sterile exercise. Unless you perform it within the context of full and extensive knowledge of, and sensitivity to, the actual setting, it will reveal little or nothing. Arbitrary box building is not a substitute for a close feel for the actual circumstances. Typologizing is simply a tool to aid in systematic understanding. (1984, p. 96)

Despite their value, typologies actually can prevent understanding if they are used inappropriately. This can happen when we attach labels to individuals that are simplistic or misleading. In his study of homeless women, for example, Liebow (1994) was careful to avoid this problem. He writes,

> In general, I have tried to avoid labeling any of the women as "mentally ill," "alcoholic," "drug addicted," or any other characterization that is commonly used to describe—or, worse, to explain—the homeless person. Judgments such as these are almost always made against a background of homelessness. If the same person were seen in another setting, the judgment might be altogether different. Like you, I know people who drink, people who do drugs, and bosses who have tantrums and treat their subordinates like dirt. They all have good jobs. Were they to become homeless, some of them would surely also become "alcoholics," or "mentally ill." Similarly, if some of the homeless women who are now so labeled were to be magically transported to a more usual and acceptable setting, some of them—not all, of course—would shed their labels and take their places with the rest of us somewhere on the spectrum of normality. (p. xiii)

Although you might find that classification schemes are extremely useful devices for differentiation and understanding, in your quest for categorization take care not to ignore other factors equally important in the lives of those we study. For example, a woman with a mental illness might also be a mother, a college professor, a first-generation immigrant from Puerto Rico, and a resident of a small town in Appalachia. When as a researcher you create a typology too quickly, often based solely on obvious differences, you run the risk of missing other factors or the intersection of factors that might be greater sources for understanding and meaning.

Another danger inherent in classification schemes is that they are too easily confused with causal factors. Russell (1991) made this point in her study of homeless women. Although in her chapter, "The Paths to Homelessness," Russell classifies the women into three types, "mentally ill," "substance abusers," and "situationally homeless," she carefully warns the reader against using classifications that carry "simplistic notions of both causation and 'cures' for homelessness" (p. 30). She does not imply, for example, that being mentally ill caused the women to be homeless. Rather, she focuses on how the factors that lead to homelessness are experienced by women with mental illnesses.

With these caveats in mind, let's begin our exploration of typologies with an example. After a full year of observing men who bet on horses at racetracks, John Rosecrance (1990) created a typology of gamblers:

1. Pros—the professional handicappers, reserved for the small percentage who have proven they can win consistently.

2. Serious players—those who have made a definite and demonstrable commitment to earn their livelihood from wagering on horses. They quit their regular jobs and begin playing the horses as a full-time endeavor.

3. Bustouts—the individuals who exist in a continuing state of poverty. In racing argot they are "permanent residents of tap city."

4. Regulars—their employment situation allows them to attend the races during the week because they are either retired or flexibly employed.

5. Part-time players—include players who are unable to attend regularly. Most of them have traditional weekly employment; they envision that after they retire they will become regulars. (pp. 359–365)

Although Rosecrance's work is a good example of a typology, it still raises a question: *How does one create a typology?* The first step in creating a typology is to determine your domain of interest; that is, *what* is it that you want to classify? Are you interested in creating a typology of types of people (professors), objects (textbooks), behaviors (studying habits), language (academic jargon), or reasons (justifications for cheating) (Spradley, 1980)? Rosecrance, as noted above, was interested in gamblers.

The second step is to ask relevant questions while coding the data. Spradley (1980) has identified nine questions that can serve as the basis for creating categories:

1. Is X a kind of Y?

2. Is X a part of Y?

3. Is X a result of Y?

4. Is X a reason for doing Y?

5. Is X a place for doing Y?

6. Is X used for Y?

7. Is X a way to do Y?

8. Is X a step in doing Y?

9. Is X a characteristic of Y? (p. 93)

During coding, researchers systematically ask the relevant question for their domain of interest. Rosecrance (1990) may have coded looking for characteristics that distinguished different *kinds* of gamblers (question 1). Alternatively, he might have wanted to organize the motivations for gambling, so during his coding he may have searched for different *reasons* for gambling (question 4).

The third step is to determine whether the relevant data can be organized into categories, often based on more than one characteristic. In the language of positivism, a typology often is based on the cross-tabulation of at least two variables. For example, Rosecrance (1990) focused, in part, on the incomes earned and employment status of the gamblers as ways of distinguishing among the different kinds of gamblers.

Again, questions help identify key features useful for classifying. Are there important characteristics that distinguish this *kind* of "Y" from that *kind* of "Y"? In what ways is this gambler different from that one? Are these two gamblers like a third? How are these *reasons* the same or different from those *reasons?* Do certain kinds of gamblers justify their gambling with different reasons? This process continues until all the relative data are compared. Unless all the people, places, reasons, and so on are unique, which would be surprising, the researcher can then classify the data into a manageable number of discrete categories.

The fourth step in creating a typology is assigning meaningful labels to the various categories—"Pros," "Serious players," "Bustouts," "Regulars," and "Part-time players." The researcher can use the labels to facilitate the discussion of the categories.

The fifth step is the presentation of the typology in the final manuscript. A discussion of a typology usually includes a description of each category, comparison across groups, and implications of the categories for understanding the participants and setting.

A key feature of a typology is that the categories have to be mutually exclusive. That is, a case (individual, object, event, reason, and so on) can fit into one and only one category. A gambler who is a "Part-timer" cannot also be a "Regular."

Ideally, the groups are exhaustive—the researcher should be able to classify all cases into one of the categories. If Rosecrance's typology were exhaustive, all the gamblers would have fit into one of the five groups. Categories labeled "other," "miscellaneous," or "mixed" are often needed to incorporate all cases. Realistically, it is not always meaningful or possible to place each case into a category (Lofland & Lofland, 1995).

As you know by now, I think real-life examples are important learning aids. Thus, I return to McGuire's (1998) dissertation research on at-risk college students to illustrate how typologies can be constructed. Her work is relevant here for two reasons. First, it demonstrates that creating typologies is usually more complex than it first appears. Second, McGuire does an excellent job of explaining her justification and procedures for her typology. When engaging in field research, clear communication of *how* one arrived at the conclusions is important for evaluating the research.

As you may recall from the previous chapter, McGuire's (1998) focused coding resulted in four major categories: "perceptions of grades earned," "perceptions of studying activities," "perceptions of faculty and advisors," and "perceptions of mental engagements." For each of these categories she developed subcategories. For example, as subcategories of "perceptions of studying activities," she identified "expectations of studying" and "preferred style of studying." Each of these subcategories she divided further—"expectations," for example, was divided into "clear" and "unclear"; "preferred styles of studying" into "individual" and "group." McGuire now has a series of variables (for example, "expectations for studying") with sets of attributes for each (for example, "clear expectations" and "unclear expectations").

By separately reporting students' perceptions in these four major categories, or variables, however, McGuire (1998) tells us in her methods section that she felt as though she was depriving the students' stories of a valuable richness and complexity. At this point, she sensed that patterns varied across the four variables. McGuire explained her procedure for identifying the patterns that eventually resulted in a typology of students:

> I developed a chart for each of the students assigning a descriptive name to the characteristic of the perceptions within a particular category for a specified element of academic performance. . . . In an effort to identify possible patterns of perceptions, I assigned colors to each of the variations in student perceptions across the elements of academic performance activities and grades. For example, a student might have characteristics "blue," "green" and "orange" for studying, characteristics "purple" and "white" for grades and so on. After the color charting was complete, each student had a distinguishable color pattern. The patterns of variations of perceptions were now evident. Several students had the exact same color scheme illustrating a similar pattern of perceptions of their academic performance.
>
> Three patterns of perceptions emerged from this color-coding scheme. I labeled each pattern with a name that represents key characteristics of the perceptions associated with academic performance, "The Right to Party," "Collaborative Progress" and "Resourceful Preparation" patterns. (p. 33)

Later in her analysis, she explored, among other things, how some aspects of the program to help at-risk students benefited "The Right to Party" students but not the "Resourceful Preparation" ones. In other words, she did not just create types of students, but explained how an awareness of different groups of students has the potential of improving programs for at-risk students.

Although typologies are not theories, they can be theoretically grounded and useful in other ways. For example, the researcher who wants to develop or test a theory about why people gamble or create a program to prevent gambling might be aided by considering the diversity expressed in Rosecrance's (1990) typology. Also, because it allowed for comparisons between his typology and those of other types of gamblers, Rosecrance's work at the horse tracks contributed to a larger body of research on gambling. Educators who want to reduce the risk of dropping out of college might be well served to consider McGuire's (1998) findings.

Typologies are not the only way to classify one's data. Taxonomies are a closely related strategy.

Taxonomies

You may never have taken a botany class, but I suspect you are familiar with the logic of taxonomies. Noell, my dog, has a place in a complicated taxonomy. Noell belongs to the kingdom of Animalia, the phylum of Chordata, the class of Mammalia, the order of Carnivora, the family of Canidae, the genus of *Canis,* and the species and subspecies of *Canis lupus familiaris.* Pookey, one of my cats, shares some of categories with Noell, but she has a different family (Elidae), genus *(Felis),* and species and subspecies *(Felis silvestris catus).* Each category in this taxonomy is a subcategory of the one that preceded it. Field researchers also create taxonomies, although not always as complicated.

When researchers create a taxonomy, they pursue an analytical strategy closely related to the one used in the development of typologies. However, there is a key difference between the two strategies. Whereas typologies separate similar cases, objects, events, activities, and so on into different categories based on key features that differentiate them, taxonomies highlight hierarchical and other relationships among categories and subcategories (Ryan & Bernard, 2003). The categories of a taxonomy, as with a typology, should be mutually exclusive and ideally exhaustive. Unlike a typology, the categories in a taxonomy are ordered; they have levels.

Let's create a nonexhaustive taxonomy of motorcycles. (Creating a taxonomy from objects allows me to provide you with a straightforward example; taxonomies of the social world are often more complex.) The category of motorcycles can be divided into subcategories, such as *sport bikes, touring bikes, standards,* and *cruisers.* Touring bikes can be divided further into *luxury* or *sport touring.* Two types of *sport touring* motorcycles are the Honda ST1300 and the Ducati ST4S.

A final manuscript often represents taxonomies visually, such as shown in Figure 10.1, with branching tree diagrams or tables indicating the relationships among categories and subcategories.

To recap, whereas typologies separate similar objects into different categories based on key features that differentiate them, taxonomies show the hierarchal relationships among categories and subcategories. As noted

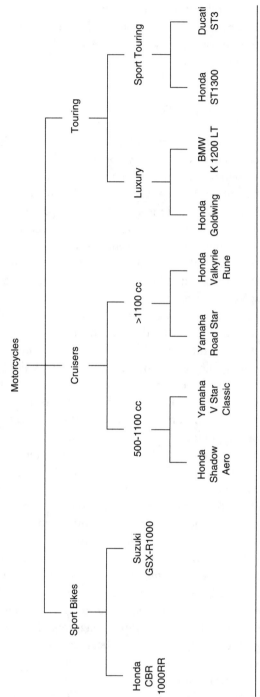

Figure 10.1 Example of a Nonexhaustive Taxonomy of Motorcycles

above, tables and diagrams are used to create typologies and taxonomies, as well as represent the completed product. The practice of creating visual representations as an analytical technique is the topic of the next section.

Visual Representations

In an effort to analyze qualitative data, researchers sometimes organize their data visually in order to gain insight into the setting and its participants. These insights can then be represented visually or textually in the final manuscript. Thus, drawings, conceptual maps, matrices, tables, and charts serve not only as visual representations of what one has learned through analysis but also as generative, analytical techniques.

Let's pretend that my field notes include a series of interactions among a group of men (Whyte, 1955). I decide to create a table to help me visually analyze the social rankings among the men. As seen below in Figure 10.2, this table lists all of the men's names. The top row of the table indicates the man who is influencing, and the first column identifies the man being influenced.

As I read my field notes, every time I find a data segment where one man influenced another, I put a check mark in the appropriate cell in the table. If this were a real project, I would also include a code that would allow me to locate where in my field notes I can find the interaction recorded.

	Mike	Danny	Doc	Angelo	Nutsy	Carl
Mike		√ √ √	√ √ √ √			
Danny	√ √ √		√√			
Doc						
Angelo		√ √ √	√ √ √ √			
Nutsy	√ √		√ √ √ √			
Carl					√	

Figure 10.2   Example of Visual Representation of Data to Facilitate Coding of the Pattern of Social Influence Among Six Men

SOURCE: Adapted from *Street corner society: The social structure of an Italian slum* (2nd ed.) (p. 13), by W. Whyte, 1955, Chicago: University of Chicago Press.

From the information in the table, I can draw conclusions regarding the patterns of interaction. Mike influenced Danny. Danny influenced Mike. Thus, Mike and Danny seem to have a fairly reciprocal interaction pattern with each other. Danny appears to have a higher status than Angelo, because he influenced him and not vice versa. The highest ranking individual seems to be Doc, who influenced everyone except for Carl and was himself influenced by no one. Carl and Angelo had no influence on any of the others. Although it took relatively little time to construct, this simple table allows me to arrive at my conclusions in a more efficient way than I could have been able to accomplish working directly and solely from the text in my field notes. Although I could describe the relative ranking in my final product, another visual representation might more easily convey my findings to readers.

Some of you might recognize my example as being drawn from some of the data from William Foote Whyte's (1955) classic ethnography of life in an economically depressed area of a large city. Whyte conveyed the relative rankings of 13 men in a simple but effective hierarchical chart, as shown in Figure 10.3.

Visual representations are useful in several ways. They serve as a method by which the researcher can simplify and make manageable complex and often intersecting bits of information. They are a means by which a researcher can literally show the results of research to an audience. The reader can often more quickly grasp the relationships among items when presented in a visual form than when described in the text.

One other comment about visuals. Collecting and analyzing visual data, graffiti, brochures, advertisements, and all kinds of photographs, are becoming increasingly common in field research. For example, both Duneier (1999) and Bourgois (1995) include powerful and illustrative photographs in their books. Although extremely useful for understanding a setting, the use of visuals is still not as common as creating themes.

Themes

In dissertation proposals, graduate students often indicate that their methodology for analyzing their data will be to find **themes** that emerge in the data. As noted in Chapter 9, I argue that researchers *create* themes from the data; themes do not simply emerge. Also, I caution against viewing themes as the only method of analysis available to researchers. Nonetheless, creating themes is a common, appropriate, and important method for analyzing data.

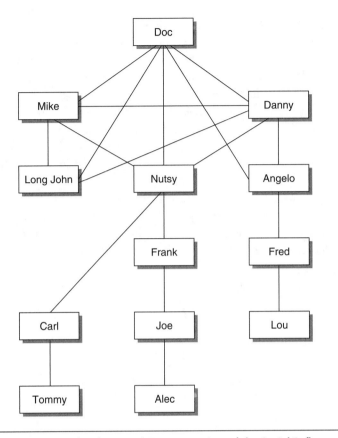

Figure 10.3   Example of a Visual Representation of the Social Influence
Among 13 Men

SOURCE: Adapted from *Street corner society: The social structure of an Italian slum* (2nd
ed.) (p. 13), by W. Whyte, copyright © 1955 by permission of University of Chicago Press.

Simply put, themes are recurring patterns, topics, viewpoints, emotions, concepts, events, and so on. They might result from things that the
researcher heard over and over. Often, themes are created during coding
as similarities across cases are identified. A theme can be an overarching
focus, such as "the theme of this section is the ways violence affects academic achievement." I will further define themes in the next chapter.

The procedures for creating themes overlap with the analytical
techniques already mentioned, yet they also possess unique features.
Typologies, by definition, require division of the domain of interest into
multiple parts or categories that are mutually exclusive. Themes, on the

other hand, can have features that overlap. Whereas categories in a taxonomy are mutually exclusive and illuminate relationships among categories, this is not always the case for themes. Themes may or may not be related. Indeed, only one theme might be sufficient for a manuscript about one's field research.

As with the other techniques, thematic analysis depends greatly on rigorous coding and recoding. In addition to performing line-by-line coding of the talk by participants, the researcher who uses thematic analysis often codes with an analytical eye toward larger segments of data. Attention to context, interactions, routine and aberrant behaviors, rhetorical conventions, and descriptions is usual for thematic analysis. That is, one can create themes from more than simply what was said.

As with so many aspects of field research, you will find that asking questions facilitates coding. Code with specific questions in mind, such as

1. What happened?

2. What led to the situation?

3. Why did it happen?

4. Who acted?

5. What preceded this event?

6. How were things resolved?

7. What was the level of emotional engagement in the interaction?

8. What were the consequences of this activity or interaction? (Strauss, 1987, pp. 27–28, as cited in Flick, 2002, p. 186)

Answers to these sorts of questions might lead you to creating useful themes.

Should you choose to pursue a thematic analysis, you start by engaging in open coding for each case separately (Flick, 2002). A case might be a transcript from one interview or field notes from one day's observations. Initially, you might find this process a bit difficult. When you code interview data, you can easily determine the parameters of a case: It would be the transcript from one person. With data from observations and interactions, however, you might experience more problems determining what sorts of boundaries should in each instance delineate a case.

After one case is coded, you review it in a search for repetitive codes. For example, did your initial coding result in multiple sections of the data being labeled "political efficacy"? If so, then you should conduct focused coding of this first case looking specifically for other instances of "political efficacy."

Once you have coded and recoded the first case, you proceed to the second case. As much as possible, code this case as if it were the first one. Once you have coded it, following the procedures for the first case, compare it with the first case. Note similarities and differences between the two cases. Revise and add codes as a result of the comparison. Comparing the two cases usually requires focused recoding of each. At this point, proceed to the third case, code it, and compare it with the first two. Follow this same procedure with each subsequent case.

By constantly comparing the data in this manner, you will begin to notice differences, as well as similarities. Why, for example, do cases one, two, and four exhibit similar routines, whereas case three reveals a different one? Seeking answers to such questions can lead you to refine your tentative conclusions or even add new ones.

As you continue coding, you will see that the tentative themes garner more support. On the one hand, this is good, because creating themes is the purpose of this kind of analysis. On the other hand, once you gain more confidence about a theme in the data, you might find it difficult to code subsequent cases with the same focused attention you paid to the first ones. Resist the urge to code only for the themes already developed from earlier cases. After all, constantly comparing does not mean simply measuring subsequent cases against earlier ones. Instead, you should revisit earlier cases on the basis of what you learned during the coding of each new one.

Thematic analyses work most effectively when you seek themes that address your research questions, frame themes conceptually, and explore links among them. A simple listing of all discernible themes without some conceptual understanding of how they fit into a larger context is like having a bunch of logs sitting side by side: They form the raw materials for a sturdy cabin, but no one would argue that they *are* a cabin. Although you might benefit from having this stack of logs, it is safe to assume that you will be better off having the completed cabin. Admittedly, not all themes are linked, and trying to create an integrated conceptual model from them is often an ideal, rather than a reality.

You can enhance the process of creating themes when you gain familiarity with the literature on your topic and have a well-developed theoretical or conceptual frame to guide your research. Common sense and personal experiences also help when you analyze the data for themes, such as expecting that child-care concerns would be present in observations of woman who have full-time careers and young children. Researchers actively comb the data for expected themes, noticing their absence as well as their presence.

Sometimes researchers code with preconceived themes in mind. Even when this occurs, however, the researcher still must code all of the data and constantly compare what he or she learns from it. More often, though, the researcher does not know what themes to expect. Chenault (2004) did not engage in her research with the expectation that one of her study's themes would involve communication problems. However, part way through her coding she began to notice data that suggested a lack of communication between representatives of the housing authority and the members of the resident council. Struggling between being excited by the thought of a new theme and being distraught over the extra effort it required, Chenault appropriately followed the procedures for a thematic analysis and returned to the data that she had coded previously, searching each line for references that might relate to communication.

When you code themes, keep in mind one element that could make your task a bit more difficult: Often, participants will not use the same terminology as you, the researcher. For example, the participants in Chenault's (2004) study did not say such things as, "One communication problem we have is that we are not getting the fliers that announce events." Rather, they talked about such problems as the mess from fliers blowing around in their yards. In fact, the first time Chenault coded her data, she did not code the fliers as being related to communication. Instead, she coded the statement about fliers blowing in yards as an example of social disorganization, a category that included items such as overflowing trash bins and lawns that needed to be mowed. However, when she revisited her data with the goal of coding instances of potential communication problems, she identified the fliers blowing around, rather than being delivered or posted appropriately, as a possible explanation for the lack of communication about community events.

When you undertake thematic analysis, you need to determine how you will present your themes. One common method is to describe the theme and then provide verbatim quotations or sections from the field notes that illustrate the theme. Researchers frequently use this presentation style for data collected through interviews. If you use this style, though, make sure that you identify the speaker, usually with a pseudonym. Otherwise, the reader has no way of knowing if all of your quotations are from one person, a few, or lots of people.

In a study of how Vietnamese-American adolescents perceived themselves in relation to their families, Phan (2005) used this approach to present themes. One theme presented was "Family Ties." Phan began the discussion of family ties with a brief summary of the literature and then continued with quotations:

> Phoung described her family involvement: "I visit my aunts, uncles, and my grandparents. I take my grandparents to the Buddhist temple when I have time on Sunday. I try to make time for my grandparents." Don offered the analysis of his feelings and relationships with his family: "We have a close relationship; my dad and I are really close." (p. 431)

After a relatively lengthy quotation by Khoa, Phan continues,

> Quan expressed a similar theme: "My parents are very important to me. I appreciate their guidance and their disciplines. I really appreciate their advice. I love both of them equally. I feel obligated to do well for them and for our honor, as well as for myself. My family is the main motivator along with our Vietnamese history. I like to learn Vietnamese history." And Giang commented: "I discuss schoolwork with my parents. I don't hide anything from them. I can't stand hiding or being secretive to my parents. If I have concerns, I will tell my parents. I need my parents' input. I value their advice." Likewise Binh commented: "Family is important. My family provides me emotional and moral support. I appreciate the values they have taught me." (p. 431)

Other themes Phan (2005) presented in the study were "Separation/ Connection" and "Cultural and Religious Values," for which the researcher used a similar presentation style.

One difficulty in presenting themes is deciding how much data one should include to illustrate a theme. The only answer to the question, *how many quotations and how long should they be?* is: It depends. It depends upon the complexity of the theme, how many members expressed the theme, the number of themes included in the manuscript, and so on. As a starting place, consider including a minimum of three quotations for each theme. Also, indicate why a particular quotation was included. For example, did you select a quotation because it was articulate, emotional, and dramatic? Did the quotation provide a slightly different view on the theme? Did you decide to use quotations that support a theme from participants who have different roles in the setting?

A common mistake in early drafts of a thematic analysis is to include a quotation from each member that relates to a particular theme. Too often, the theme is described in a sentence or two followed by several pages of quotations that essentially all say the same thing. An improved presentation is one with increased attention to flushing out the theme and its analytical importance followed by selected quotations. I suggest that you avoid being too "quotatious," a term I use to refer to the overuse of long quotations or the use of more information than is relevant. Deciding what is relevant often is easier than deciding how long a quotation should be. In most cases a paragraph of information is sufficient. You are in the danger zone if you produce several pages of quotations without including the sort of contextual narrative that will help your reader understand their significance.

In contrast to using small segments of data to support a theme, sometimes pages of material from observations, field notes, and taped transcripts might be necessary to illustrate a theme. Duneier (1999) has 74 pages devoted to what could be called his theme of "The Limits of Informal Social Control" (p. 54). He uses four examples, each a chapter, to illustrate this theme—"Sidewalk Sleeping," "When You Gotta Go," "Talking to Women," and "Accusations: Caveat Vendor??"

One potential pitfall of a thematic analysis is only seeking and presenting data that supports the expressed theme of the research, a problem that can lead readers to the unfounded conclusion that most participants expressed the theme. When you produce a thematic analysis, clarify for readers who did (and did not, if relevant) make reference to the theme. Sometimes, researchers include **frequencies** so as not to mislead the reader. For example, a researcher might indicate that eight of ten men interviewed made statements consistent with the theme. As with some of the other analytical techniques presented in this chapter, an analysis of cases that did not express the explicit theme of your research often provides insight into the setting.

Typologies, taxonomies, visual representations, and themes are ways of classifying data. Storytelling, an analytical strategy presented in the next chapter, incorporates thematic analysis.

Chapter Highlights

1. Field researchers use the construction of types, typologies, visual representations, and taxonomies as analytical aids.

2. When used incorrectly, typologies can misrepresent the complexity of social life.

3. Typologies and taxonomies should not be confused with causes.

4. Asking and answering questions during the coding process help in the construction of typologies and taxonomies.

5. Typologies organize data into mutually exclusive categories based on sets of key characteristics.

6. Taxonomies organize categories of data by the hierarchical relationships among them.

7. Diagrams, maps, flowcharts, organizational charts, and other visual representations are useful tools for analyzing data.

8. Themes result from carefully coding the data by constantly comparing cases for similarities and differences.

9. A thematic analysis is at its strongest when the themes are conceptual categories and relationships among themes are explored.

10. Themes are often presented with quotations or excerpts from field notes to illustrate them.

Exercises

1. Collect the front page of a local newspaper for five days in a row. Using scissors, floor space, and anything else you need, organize all the articles into meaningful groups. Create a typology of the articles. Describe your typology and the procedures you used to create it. Discuss what you learned about the priorities in the news after creating your typology.

2. Interview 15 people about their views on college football. Create and describe a typology of football fans based on their responses. The better your interview questions, the easier this exercise will be to complete.

3. Find two academic journal articles that include a typology or taxonomy. Summarize each of the author's arguments about the contribution of the classification scheme for our understanding of the subject matter of the articles.

4. Pick a public setting that is relatively busy, but one that does not serve food or drinks, and observe the first 15 people who enter the location. For example, a local public library, a laundromat, a place that rents videos, or a small convenience or clothing store all meet the criteria. Although you are not required to obtain informed consent in public settings such as these, you most likely will need the permission of an owner, staff, or employee in some settings. Make sure that you do not complete this exercise in a way that makes anyone feel uncomfortable, as this would be unethical.

Create one or more maps of the location. Then, diagram the traffic pattern of the participants from the time they enter the setting until they leave. That is, indicate on your map(s) if they enter and go directly to the current releases or the comedy section. Is the sale rack hunted for and browsed before other items? You need to collect the data by drawing on your map(s), rather than describing their behavior in textual form. Based on your visual representation, describe what might be a typical pattern of the participants. Then describe at least one divergent pattern. Discuss what was easy and difficult about this task.

5.   Interview 15 people about their views on sports. Create and discuss themes based on their responses. Include appropriate quotations. The better your interview questions, the easier this exercise will be to complete.

11

Storytelling, Critical Events, and Analytic Induction

This chapter presents three additional techniques for analyzing data: storytelling, critical event analysis, and analytic induction. As before, these strategies overlap with each other and with those presented in earlier chapters. The chapter ends with brief comments on interpreting the results of an analysis.

Storytelling

"Once upon a time" (Grimm & Grimm, 1955), "It was a dark and stormy night" (Bulwer-Lytton, 1830), and "Call me Ishmael" (Melville, 1851) are easily recognized beginnings to a fairy tale and novels. "Hakim Hasan is a book vendor and street intellectual at the busy intersection of Eight Street, Greenwich Avenue, and the Avenue of the Americas—aka Sixth Avenue" (Duneier, 1999, p. 3), and "I was forced into crack against my will" (Bourgois, 1995, p. 1) are lesser known opening lines to two of the ethnographies often cited in this guide. Although later we learn that Bourgois is referring to the necessity of including in his book an analysis of the role of drugs in "El Barrio," he grabbed my attention with his very first sentence. These researchers know how to tell a good story.

Creating stories provides researchers—particularly those who produce books based upon their fieldwork—with yet another way to analyze and present data. Creating **stories** usually requires the researcher to incorporate other analytical techniques, such as descriptions and themes, but these are not in and of themselves stories. Additionally, although what members of a setting say is important to most stories, their responses to the researcher's questions do not always contain stories. I suggest that field researchers can gain insight into a setting and participants by organizing the data in such a way as to create a compelling story. Although the elements of a story obviously are embedded in the data, they lie dormant until the researcher crafts them into something meaningful.

This chapter focuses on *creating stories* or *creating narratives* as a way of analyzing data. The technique discussed here is not about the analysis *of* stories. Although I refer, at times, to the creation of narratives as a narrative analysis, other researchers reserve the term **narrative analysis** to refer to the procedures for analyzing the stories, or narratives, told *by* the participants. When used in this sense, a narrative analysis might focus on how the participants' stories are organized, the rhetoric with which they are told, why they are being told, and their major themes (Esterberg, 2002; Schwandt, 2001). Researchers might engage in a particular type of interview, the narrative interview, to specifically elicit stories from respondents. The participant is asked to tell a story about a significant event in his or her life, for example (Schwandt, 2001).

There are other, conflicting definitions of the term narrative analysis, and disagreements exist over whether narratives and stories are the same thing (Esterberg, 2002). Complex methods for analyzing stories, narratives, talk, and conversations also come from traditions of discourse analysis, conversational analysis, and literary analysis. How one might go about analyzing what participants say might depend upon one's disciplinary training and the focus of one's research. For example, an individual sentence might be worthy of detailed attention rather than the structure of a lengthy story.

I am not, however, using the term narrative analysis to refer to analyzing stories. In this discussion, I refer to a narrative analysis as a procedure for crafting a story from the events in the setting. Thus, the stories that result from the analysis are firmly grounded in the data. A narrative is also a way of presenting data.

Ignoring the important and not-so-important conflicting definitions and meanings, in the following discussion, I interchangeably use the terms *telling a story, narrative analysis,* and *creating a narrative.* Moreover, I use *narrative* and *story* as equivalent nouns. However, I remind you that not everyone will find my use and blending of the terms appropriate.

Those of you who have written short stories, either for pleasure or for a creative writing class, probably already know that telling a story is more difficult than it first appears (Esterberg, 2002), and this is equally the case for field researchers. A key difference between a fictional short story and a field research narrative is that the former springs from the writer's imagination, whereas the latter has its genesis in the lives of the participants in the setting. Yet, fictional stories and field research stories share many of the same requirements.

Plots

Every story requires a plot, and a plot requires actions. Unlike the action in a movie of that genre—which might focus on car chases, fight scenes, and well-timed explosions—the action in a narrative does not have to be writ large. On the contrary, it can be quite subtle, yet nonetheless revelatory. The astute researcher can find action in the smallest snippet of everyday life in a setting, just as long as something transpires, unfolds, occurs, or happens. Otherwise, no story exists, because no "forward" movement occurs.

However, actions or events in and of themselves do not make a plot. A plot includes arranging a series of events such that they reveal the "what, how, and why" (Burroway, 2003, p. 45). As an example, "the king died and then the queen died" is a description of two events. In contrast, "the king died and then the queen died of grief" is a plot line because it tells us that the queen died *because* of her grief from the king's death (Burroway, 2003). Thus, when creating stories, the researcher uses the careful coding of data to try to get at *why* the events observed transpired as they did. Articulating the meaningful relationships among events moves the analysis beyond description.

Characters

Stories cannot exist without characters to populate them. In field research, characters come in many shapes and forms: They are the participants in the setting, others talked about by participants, or people observed by the researcher. Even the researcher can be a character, particularly in fieldwork guided by interpretive or critical paradigms.

A common goal of field research is to understand a setting from the perspectives of the participants, or characters in the parlance of creative writing. This goal is largely unobtainable if the researcher and eventually the readers of the final manuscript do not *know* the participants (Burroway, 2003, p. 157). Burroway's suggestions for characterization in a short story apply to a narrative analysis:

1. Know the characters' appearance and body language, and where they are and what is around them.

2. Know the details of the characters' lives—their routine and not so routine behaviors.

3. Identify inconsistencies and patterns in their talk, appearance, and behaviors.

4. Examine their speech—not just content but how and when it is said and the meanings behind it. (p. 180)

Burroway's suggestions should sound familiar because in earlier chapters in this guide I stressed the importance of writing thick descriptions, making keen observations, having detailed field notes, and taping interviews. You will be happy that you followed this advice if you attempt to craft a story from your data.

Characters do not exist in a vacuum. Rather, their experiences are grounded in a particular place and time.

Place and Time

Place and time are essential elements of a story and not just merely a stage on which a play is performed. The story's setting is so infused with the plot and characters that to talk about them separately is misleading.

Two of my favorite authors, Lisa Norris and Arundhati Roy, begin their works by establishing elements of place and time. Norris begins her story:

> When they first walked in, the emptiness of the place made sense to Cory. After all, it was late September in Alaska. Winter could begin anytime. (2000, p. 9)

Roy's first line is:

> May in Ayemenem is a hot, brooding month. The days are long and humid. (1997, p. 3)

Without knowing anything else, would you guess that the events about to unfold in the two stories would be the same if the months were July and December? Probably not. Would the characters that inhabit Norris's story have the same experiences if they were suddenly transported from Alaska to Ayemenem? We can turn to Eudora Welty (1994), a well-known Southern writer, for the answer to this question:

> Every story would be another story, and unrecognizable if it took up its characters and plot and happened somewhere else. . . . Fiction depends for its life on place. Place is the crossroads of circumstance, the proving ground of, What happened? Who's here? Who's coming?

Settings matter, whether "El Barrio," Sixth Avenue, Hogwarts, or a homeless shelter. Yet, not everything about the setting is crucial for our understanding. Thus, during a narrative analysis, part of the analytical task is to determine *which* features of the setting are integral to the story.

The element of time is important not only to the unfolding of events in the field, but also to how stories are told. Because most participants tend not to relate potential stories in one neatly organized narrative that follows the chronological order of the action as it occurred, researchers have to reconstruct the temporal order of events. The final manuscript can then present a story in chronological order.

Another structure for telling a story involves ending the story, then flashing back to events that preceded it, a well-known plot device in novels and film. Take, for example, the popular television series *Lost* (Abrams, 2004), which follows a group of plane crash survivors as they struggle to survive on a tropical island. Each week's installment tends to focus on a particular character, providing revelations into the person's personality and psyche through flashbacks to his or her past life.

Countless other films and television series have used the same technique. Why are flashbacks so popular? Unlike chronological presentations, those that use flashbacks consistently withhold crucial, insightful bits of information from the reader or viewer, a technique that holds the attention or captures interest because it promises to provide the answer to some mystery. In the case of *Lost,* what happened to the Southern loner that makes him reluctant to share his emotions? Why does the bold heroine Kate treasure a small toy plane? How did the former box salesman become a veritable survivalist? Narrative sequence thus plays a vital role in how the researcher—like the screenwriter, novelist, and television producer—constructs a story that will attract the readers' interest. However attractive a particular structure appears, though, the researcher always should select a format that conveys the substantive significance of the story.

Summaries and Scenes

Another way that time is relevant for storytelling is through decisions about providing summaries or presenting scenes. Condensing events that took place over a long period of time into a few paragraphs is a summary (Burroway, 2003). In contrast, a scene is a relatively lengthy account of what happened in a short amount of time. In a narrative analysis, summaries are included, but scenes are prioritized. Without scenes, there is no story (Burroway, 2003).

The goal of writing a scene is to put the readers in the setting with the members—in "real" time—as the events unfold (Burroway, 2003). The reader's response to a scene should be the feeling of being there, of listening, of observing. In contrast, the response to a summary is that someone else is providing a synopsis of events for you.

Notice how the level of intimacy changes for you as a reader in the following summary and scene. Duneier (1999) provides this summary:

> Several other elements serve to make Greenwich Village a sustaining habitat that is ideal for magazine scavenging and vending. The neighborhood is the home of many people who are sympathetic to unhoused people and are willing to give money and food to them. (p. 147)

Duneier (1999) begins the following scene by telling us that Ellen, a 50-year-old White woman, wanted to donate magazines to a vendor in exchange for a discount on a magazine she wanted:

> "You know I gotta charge full price," Marvin told her in a defiant but joking manner.
>
> "But I'm going to give you a lot of magazines!" she told him, smiling.
>
> "So you want me to take out your garbage *and* give you a discount?" Marvin retorted. "It gotta be good magazines. I gotta have an eye for them. I can't just take a whole bunch of average stuff and put it on my table."
>
> "No!" she responded. "They're all good ones. They're all ones I got from you!" (p. 147)

A major difference between these two examples is that the summary was written from Duneier's perspective. In contrast, in the scene, Duneier allowed the vendor and the woman to speak for themselves by including their dialogue.

Dialogue

Dialogue is another essential feature of a story. Once again, a difference between fiction and research is that in the former the dialogue is created by the writer and in the latter the dialogue emanates from the participants in the setting. Certainly, the field researcher has to establish rapport, ask the right questions, tape and transcribe interviews, code, and present dialogue in meaningful ways. But ultimately, the dialogue included in a narrative account is not a figment of the researcher's imagination.

Even though researchers do not have to invent dialogue, a major part of crafting a scene is deciding what and how much dialogue is needed. There are no rules to say how much or how little will suffice to advance the story. Book-length ethnographies often have multiple pages of dialogue with no authorial commentary. Quotations are often richer than paraphrases, and letting others speak for themselves is frequently better than summarizing their views. This is why, in part, I have used so many quotations and examples in this guide. I believe that it is important to retain the voices of the speakers.

Point of View

Stories are told from a point of view, possibly even multiple points of view. In the field of creative writing, the novelist or short-story writer creates point of view at will. He or she might choose the first-person narrative approach, the omniscient narrative stance, or any one of numerous other options—whichever best serves the narrative flow at any one time. Although the pieces of the narrative already exist in field notes and in the transcripts of others' spoken words, rather than being drawn from the imagination, the researcher decides whose point of view the story will reflect, a choice shaped by the paradigm he or she selects. For example, a researcher using a post-positivist paradigm might tell the story as an invisible, objective narrator. On the other hand, the researcher using an interpretive paradigm might be included as a central character in the story, comparing his or her perspective with those of the participants.

In a previous chapter, Switzer recounts her experiences drinking milk in a Maasai village. She writes, in part, "Maasai milk is really more like drinkable yogurt." In this sentence, Switzer takes the perspective of the invisible narrator telling us about the milk. Had she located herself more explicitly in the story, she might have written instead, "The Maasai milk tastes to me like a drinkable yogurt." Told from the point of view of the Maasai, Switzer might have used the words of one of the women, "Our milk is like a drinkable yogurt."

This milk example is overly simplified to the point of being misleading. Why? In each case the milk still was compared to yogurt, whereas in the "real world," stories told from different views rarely have this form of agreement. The narrative style of telling divergent points of view, even when voices ostensibly tell the same story, is referred to as *Rashomon,* from the title of the 1950 Japanese classic film that recounts four eyewitnesses' divergent accounts of a crime. Because of the lack of consistency in how events are experienced and told, researchers craft stories that use multiple points of view.

Regardless of the point of view, researchers have to be clear about why they are telling the story. What is the purpose, theme, or point of the story being relayed?

Themes

A discussion of themes as an element of stories in fiction and field research is not as straightforward as one would hope. Burroway (2003) notes that a theme for creative writing is often discussed in terms of what it is not: A "theme is not the *message,* not the *moral*" (p. 357). The theme, or meaning, cannot be paraphrased (p. 357). A theme is what the story is about, but it is not the plot of the story. Stories are about life and death; love and rejection; loss and gain; good and evil.

In literature, themes contain ideas, but Burroway (2003) asserts that they are not stated as ideas (p. 357). We, as readers, sometimes have to figure out the "point of the story." I recall being somewhat irritated when Mrs. Sheppard, my wonderful ninth-grade English teacher, would ask, *What do you think the author is trying to convey in this story?* I felt it was somewhat unfair of her to ask me this question if the author wasn't willing to state the theme explicitly. Now I might respond that the point of a story is dependent, in part, on the reader's response. However, field research stories should leave no one guessing about why the story was included in the final manuscript.

The craft of writing fictional stories and field research stories diverges at the point of themes. Unlike creative writers, field researchers are quite explicit about the theme of their stories. Readers are often told the theme before the scene, and its relevance to larger issues might be clearly articulated afterwards as well.

Determining the theme of the story being crafted is the most difficult part of this kind of analysis. Indeed, it is through careful coding of the data that the utility of a narrative analysis becomes clear. And through the task of writing preliminary drafts of a story, the point is often determined by the researcher, much like the first draft of an essay in which one discovers the thesis sentence on the last page. Sometimes, however, the researcher abandons the story if it serves no purpose. If stories don't shed light on the research questions, they might not be worth telling. It is during the narrative analysis where this decision is made.

The Final Story

When all decisions are made and the narrative analysis is completed, the results should be a compelling story that provides readers with insight into the lives of the participants in the setting. I return to Welty (1994) to summarize the art of storytelling:

> This makes it the business of writing, and the responsibility of the writer, to disentangle the significant—in character, incident, setting, mood, everything—from the random and meaningless and irrelevant that in real life surround and beset it. It is a matter of his selecting and, by all that implies, of changing "real" life as he goes. With each word he writes, he acts as literally and methodically as if he hacked his way through a forest and blazed it for the word that follows. He makes choices at the explicit demand of this one present story; each choice implies, explains, limits the next, and illuminates the one before.

Extended Example

Given that beginning researchers often equate "finding themes" with data analysis, I use an extended example from Duneier's (1999) research on street vendors to demonstrate the narrative as an alternative analytic and presentation style. In a section of his book titled "Limits of Informal Social Control," he introduces the difficulties the men have in gaining access to public restrooms to illustrate his larger conceptual point that formal social controls have, at times, exacerbated rather than reduced problems, primarily because they often undermine effective informal ones already in place.

He begins the chapter by noting that because the setting in question—Sixth Avenue—has no public restrooms, the street vendors who work there often are left with little choice but to urinate against the side of buildings. After thus contextualizing his story and foreshadowing its point, he tells it:

> "I gotta get me a paper cup and I'm gonna be all right," Mudrick tells me as we walk down Sixth Avenue at 10:00 p.m. After he finds one in a trashcan, he pauses, unzips his pants, and begins urinating into it. I ask him why.
>
> "This is for the street, Mitch. This is for Guiliano," he laughs, referring to the mayor, who is more commonly known as Rudolph Giuliani. "Guiliano say you can't go to the bathroom. I invented this thing. Now everybody out here gets a cup. You can't go to the bathroom in the stores and restaurants, because they don't want you in there if you ain't got no money to spend. So how you gonna piss? You gotta get a cup."
>
> "And then you just throw it in the street?" I ask.
>
> "Throw it in the street!" said Mudrick.
>
> "And that's for Giuliani?" I ask, surprised that urination is being described as a political act.
>
> "Yeah. I went to Riker's Island jail for pissing in the street. Now I get a cup." (Duneier, 1999, pp. 173–174)

Two paragraphs later, the story continues:

> A few days earlier, I had noticed Mudrick flagging down a cab. None stopped for him. A few seconds later, he turned away with a cup in hand and dumped it in the sewer. While Mudrick pretends to be hailing a cab, he holds the cup and urinates under an untucked shirt. . . .
>
> On another occasion, after dumping his urine in the sewer, Mudrick placed the Starbucks cup he had just used on the branch of a tree on Sixth Avenue.
>
> (The tree had been planted by the local Business Improvement District to cut down on space for vendors.) I had occasionally noticed paper cups hanging from tree branches but had never thought twice about them. (p. 174)

After Duneier presents Mudrick's solution to the bathroom problem, he then turns to the stories of Ron and Raj. Although he notes similarities and differences among the three men, the men's voices remain as Duneier relates large segments of the conversations he had with them about the lack of places to urinate. Duneier blends descriptive details about the men into his story. For example, about Raj he tells us:

> While Ron and I were talking, Raj, the Indian worker in the corner newsstand shack at Sixth and Waverly Place walked up and greeted us. He was dressed in his Italian silk slacks, ironed cotton shirt, and tennis shoes; he was well groomed and had the appearance of a man who had showered earlier in the day. Since he also worked on Sixth Avenue and had no bathroom inside his newsstand, I asked if he engages in similar behavior.
>
> "Let me ask you a question: when you are in your newsstand and you have to urinate, where do you go?"
>
> "I go over there," Raj said, pointing to Baluchis, the Indian restaurant across the street, at Sixth and Washington Place. He says that, when he is in the newsstand by himself and can't get away, he "makes it" in a cup and puts it in a garbage can. (pp. 177–178)

Not all research projects prove amenable to the act of storytelling. But when appropriate, I think stories provide a richness that other forms of data presentation often lack. For example, an overreliance on themes that are illustrated only by quotations can rob field research of much of its power. Both formats can convey some of the same information, but a narrative analysis prioritizes the participants. When an analytical style focuses on what is said disconnected from the speaker, the context gets lost, the observational data are not as apt to be included with the speech, and the presence of the researcher disappears—all features that often help make field research more insightful than interview data.

I am championing storytelling as a method of analysis because over the years of serving on many graduate committees and teaching undergraduate courses, I have found this the single best way to teach the analysis of field data. Students who use this technique tend to write manuscripts that are more detailed and conceptually stronger than when employing other strategies. I suspect that this might be the case because writing stories based on the data is frankly more fun. Possibly because of this, students become more immersed in their data, better able to draw out the theoretical, conceptual, and disciplinary implications of their work. Within the course of writing their story, they often use other techniques of analyzing their data that they first found intimidating. Also, when students do not know how to start their analysis and are frozen in place as a result, I suggest that they begin with "once upon a time." By starting with a familiar line from their youth, they usually gain the momentum to write a rigorous final manuscript of high quality.

Critical Events

A **critical event analysis** is closely related to a narrative analysis, but it typically has a much smaller focus. Further, a critical event analysis does not require all the elements of a story needed for a narrative analysis. Wolcott (1994) reminds us that because no researcher can ever tell the "whole story," a solution is to select a particular event or activity and subject it to microscopic scrutiny.

Ideal events are ones that "perfectly capture" the essence (themes, characteristics, relationships, patterns) of the whole (Wolcott, 1994, p. 19). Oddly enough, clichés, idioms, or other trite sayings might help you think about critical events. Critical events are ones that "just say it all"—like finding out your friend's boyfriend hit her. A larger story about why she broke up with him could be told. However, once we know about this pivotal moment, we might not need more to understand why she terminated the relationship. Critical events are moments when things started "spiraling out of control," such as when a classmate decided to cheat on a sociology exam. Possibly you kissed a close friend and "everything changed after that." Maybe problems among the roommates "all came to a head" the night that one of them threw an impromptu party. Critical events "provide a window into a larger world."

Placing your focused attention on a particular event is what Wolcott calls "doing less more thoroughly" (Wolcott, 1990, p. 62, as cited in Wolcott, 1994). Events selected for this kind of analysis are varied; they can be activities that have great significance to the members or ones that dramatically change the trajectory of the daily life in a setting. Alternatively, they can be something seemingly "uneventful" that has implications for or is illustrative of processes occurring on a much wider scale.

Wolcott's (1994) work provides a good example of critical event analysis. As part of a larger case study of an elementary school principal, Wolcott included detailed accounts of the Principal Selection Committee as a critical event because "that event, though well removed from the daily routine of any principal, *brought into bold relief* several aspects central to the professional life of the case study principal and to the principals with which he worked" [italics added] (p. 140). After analyzing the committee meetings, Wolcott concluded that within them one could find evidence of three interrelated dimensions of the principal's life and work: the lack of professional knowledge associated with the role, an esteem for personal feelings, and a proclivity toward variety-reducing behavior (p. 14).

Likewise, along with other analytical techniques, in her study of a public housing community, Chenault (2004) used critical event analysis, focusing her attention on an episode she aptly identified as the "grass incident." One member of the resident council expressed concern that, because the grass in the community had remained uncut for so long, snakes had moved into the yards and posed a safety hazard for the children who played there. Although the resident's request that the grass be mowed seems so simple and reasonable that one might expect it to have been implemented quickly, this was not the case. During this "grass incident," issues of self-determination, power, inadequate funding, gender relations, employee turnover, and disjunctions between the written policies of the community and tenant expectations surfaced. In her presentation of the struggle over mowing the grass, Chenault appropriately used critical event analysis to demonstrate how seemingly diverse issues coalesced in such a way as to hinder improvements in the community.

Similarly, in her ethnography of a banguay (village) in the Philippines, Macabuac (2005) used the collection of oysters by female inhabitants as a critical event for purposes of her analysis. Guided by world systems and eco-feminist theories, she demonstrated in her detailed narrative of the oyster collection process how global policies played out at the micro level. Macabuac made vivid for readers the fact that export food production had created such ecological destruction for the banguay that oysters had become an important food source for the inhabitants, a food that required long hours of backbreaking labor by the women.

A close cousin to a critical event analysis is a **critical case analysis** that focuses the researcher's attention on a single individual. Concentrating on one case in depth allows for highly detailed accounts of how one person navigates the complex web of social relationships, processes, and structures in the setting.

In her ethnography of a grassroots organization in New York City that defended the legal and human rights of the city's Mexican immigrants, Solis (2003) embedded just such a critical case. She used theories of sociohistory and dialectical violence to examine how Mexican youths become victimized by their illegal status. In addition to a thematic analysis that addressed how Mexican youths experience, understand, and discuss illegality, she explored what kinds of violence they face. Solis included a critical case study of a single youth, David, to illustrate how multiple kinds of violence intersect with an individual's identity formation (p. 23). Through a highly detailed analysis of David's experiences, she provided insight into how the status of illegality "produced on a societal level through social structures such as the mass media, immigration laws, and popular opinion" plays out at the level of the individual (p. 16).

Certainly many researchers have a different goal than understanding the implications of critical events or cases. Some of these researchers give primacy to conceptual modeling.

Analytic Induction

Some researchers choose **analytic induction** as a technique for analyzing field data. Defining the term is tricky business because different meanings and procedures for it abound in the literature. Analytic induction overlaps with other techniques, making it difficult to define as a unique form of analysis (Ryan & Bernard, 2003).

Because this guide lacks sufficient space to review all of the complexities of analytic induction, I will highlight only two of its main features. First, researchers often use analytic induction in the development of conceptual models, including causal ones. Those analyzing the data might pose hypotheses during the procedure and then support, reject, or modify them as the analysis continues. Second, moreso than other techniques, analytic induction emphasizes the search for negative cases.

Analytic induction involves five distinct steps. The first involves choosing the phenomena to be explained (Flick, 1999; Ryan & Bernard, 2003). The second step involves the researcher proposing an explanation or model, possibly drawn from the literature. The researcher might then derive a hypothesis from the model.

During the third step, the researcher begins coding the data, one case at a time. For example, a case might be an individual's response to an interview question. Thus, the researcher would start coding the first interviewee's answer to the question. The purpose of the coding is to determine whether the data from the first case are consistent with the posed explanation or hypothesis. If the data from the first case support the explanation or hypothesis, then the researcher turns to the next case, repeating the procedure until he or she discovers an instance, called a **negative case,** that refutes the hypothesis.

Locating a negative case leads to the fourth step. In light of the negative case, the researcher either modifies the proposed hypothesis or model so it can accommodate the new case or, should this prove impossible, abandons the tentative explanation. The final step continues this process of supporting and refining one's conceptual model until a universal explanation is found (Flick, 1999; Ryan & Bernard, 2003).

Wolburg's (2001) study of how college students perceive the risks of binge drinking provides an example of analytic induction. Her work begins with three explanatory models often used for explaining risky behaviors—the Protection Motivation Theory, the Extended Parallel Process Model, and the Health Belief Model. Using analytic induction, Wolburg eventually creates a new, integrated model of risky behavior, the Integrated Risk Perception Model, that contains elements from the others. As is often the case with analytic induction, she provides a visual representation of her findings, as shown in Figure 11.1.

Interpretation

Storytelling, critical event analysis, and analytic induction are three of many strategies that can help you gain insight into your setting and its participants. Regardless of the analytic strategy employed, however, the goal remains to understand the experiences and meanings attached to them from the perspectives of the participants, realizing that the understanding will be mediated by the researchers' views, skills, conceptual framework, and choices made. When analyzing your data, you will find that there are no substitutes for hard work, thinking, reflection, writing, talking, and immersing yourself in the setting. Still, I agree with Jorgensen that the best strategy for analytic insight is to "Use your imagination! The analysis of data leading to discovery requires creativity" (1989, p. 110).

Creativity plays its most important role in field research during the interpretation of the data, the process by which you build on and extend what you learned during your analysis. Wolcott (1994) asserts that the goal of interpretation is "to reach out for understanding or explanation beyond the limits of what can be explained with the degree of certainty usually associated with analysis" (pp. 10–11). During the interpretive process, the researcher attempts to answer the key questions, such as, *What*

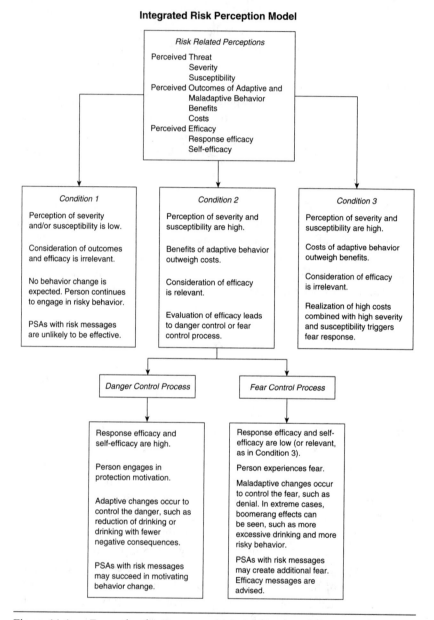

Integrated Risk Perception Model

Risk Related Perceptions

Perceived Threat
    Severity
    Susceptibility
Perceived Outcomes of Adaptive and
    Maladaptive Behavior
    Benefits
    Costs
Perceived Efficacy
    Response efficacy
    Self-efficacy

Condition 1

Perception of severity and/or susceptibility is low.

Consideration of outcomes and efficacy is irrelevant.

No behavior change is expected. Person continues to engage in risky behavior.

PSAs with risk messages are unlikely to be effective.

Condition 2

Perception of severity and susceptibility are high.

Benefits of adaptive behavior outweigh costs.

Consideration of efficacy is relevant.

Evaluation of efficacy leads to danger control or fear control process.

Condition 3

Perception of severity and susceptibility are high.

Costs of adaptive behavior outweigh benefits.

Consideration of efficacy is irrelevant.

Realization of high costs combined with high severity and susceptibility triggers fear response.

Danger Control Process

Fear Control Process

Response efficacy and self-efficacy are high.

Person engages in protection motivation.

Adaptive changes occur to control the danger, such as reduction of drinking or drinking with fewer negative consequences.

PSAs with risk messages may succeed in motivating behavior change.

Response efficacy and self-efficacy are low (or relevant, as in Condition 3).

Person experiences fear.

Maladaptive changes occur to control the fear, such as denial. In extreme cases, boomerang effects can be seen, such as more excessive drinking and more risky behavior.

PSAs with risk messages may create additional fear. Efficacy messages are advised.

Figure 11.1   Example of a Conceptual Model Developed Using Analytic Induction

SOURCE: From "The 'risky business' of binge drinking among college students: Using risk models for PSAs and anti-drinking campaigns." *Journal of Advertising, 30*, p. 36, by J. Wolberg, 2001. Adapted by permission.

is important about this research? and *Why should anyone care?* When interpreting their analytical material, researchers draw inferences, use theory for insights, raise questions, make comparisons, and provide personal reactions. Interpretation requires hunches, insights, and intuition (Creswell, 1998; Wolcott, 1994).

As you might guess, interpreting data is as difficult, usually more so, as analyzing it. Indeed, the difficulty is such that Wolcott (1994) suggests that beginning researchers should favor analytical descriptions over interpretive accounts, not necessarily the best advice for graduate students.

The interpretation of the data can be included with the analysis section of a final manuscript; indeed, some scholars view analysis and interpretations as one and the same. Others view them as separate processes (Wolcott, 1994). Under this condition, common for dissertations, the interpretations are often reserved for the last chapter.

The last chapter is often the most difficult one to write. Instead of being all excited about the moment when one can tell the reader, *this is what it means and why it is important,* burnout has probably set in. Drafts of final chapters often read like the quotation attributed to Peter Sellers, "And in conclusion, I just say this" (ThinkExist.com, 2005)—a sentence that promises more than is delivered. Once again, I suggest that beginning researchers move beyond their solitary pursuit and call on the expertise of others through returning to the literature and frequent interactions with committee members and instructors. This is a common practice among researchers, and one that can help with the interpretive process. Once the interpretation section of the research is drafted, the researcher can move on to making more decisions about the final manuscript.

Chapter Highlights

1. Creating narrative accounts, or stories, is a useful technique for gaining insight into a setting and its members.

2. Stories must have plots, characters, places, times, dialogue, scenes, points of view, and themes.

3. Writing stories is a way for the researcher to "place" the reader into the setting as events unfold; the reader is "there," experiencing what occurred, and is not simply being given a summary of events.

4. Researchers engage in critical event analysis and critical case analysis to provide a microscopic view of how processes of the whole play out in specific instances.

5. Analytic induction is a useful technique for developing conceptual models.

Exercises

---

1.   Identify all the elements of a story that Duneier includes in his story about men and urination.

2.   Take field notes about your activities during a typical day for you. Create themes, as I described in Chapter 10, from the data in your notes. Write about your day using themes as your style of presentation. Include snippets from your field notes that illustrate each theme. Then, using the same field notes, write a story about your activities. Which technique provides your readers with the most insight into a typical day for you? Justify your answer. Which format did you prefer writing?

3.   Write a one-page narrative about something that happened to you as a child. Then, write at least one paragraph that discusses *why* this event was important. That is, what makes this event significant enough that you selected it from all your childhood memories? Discuss what this exercise has to do with what was presented in this chapter.

12

Evaluation Criteria and Final Manuscript

Sooner or later, all good things must come to an end, and the same holds true for field research. You have formulated important research questions and rigorously planned and implemented a methodology designed to bring your work to fruition. Prepared with a theoretical background and informed by reading the literature on your topic, you gathered and analyzed data, eventually drawing from it what you believe to be important conclusions. Now you confront the last and most difficult task faced by the researcher: how to incorporate your preparation, data, and analysis into a final manuscript designed to present your work and findings to an audience that will unquestionably judge the fruits of your labors.

Evaluation Criteria

Given what has been presented elsewhere in this guide, you can probably guess that some of the evaluative criteria for qualitative research depend upon the paradigm, and that even within a given paradigm, researchers do not always agree. However, regardless of the paradigm, qualitative researchers often must answer questions about the **validity, reliability**, and **generalizability** of their work.

At first glance, at least for quantitative researchers, each of these terms has a straightforward definition. *Validity* refers to studying or measuring that which one intended to study or measure. *Reliability* refers to the consistency of findings over time. *Generalizability* involves applicability of the results to the population from which the sample was drawn.

With further inspection, however, you will discover that these concepts are more complex than they first appear. For example, many types of validity exist, including **face validity, construct validity,** and **concurrent validity.** A test-retest method might be used to see if a measurement instrument is reliable over time, or inter-rater reliability could be calculated to determine whether two different observers obtained the same results. When qualitative researchers enter the discussion about validity, reliability, and generalizability, the situation gets considerably more complicated.

Imagine a group of field researchers talking about validity. One researcher argues that concerns about and definitions of validity are the same for qualitative and quantitative researchers—a "rose is a rose is a rose," as the author Gertrude Stein (1922) wrote in "Sacred Emily." In rebuttal, though, another researcher responds that she strives for trustworthiness, not validity, since validity is an evaluative criterion that isn't applicable to qualitative research. After all, to recall a song by Gershwin and Gershwin (1937), "You like potato and I like potahto. You like tomato and I like tomahto." Potatoes and potahtoes are not the same things, nor are tomatoes and tomahtoes. One should not try to substitute one for the other. To complicate matters further, a third researcher chimes in that trustworthiness *is* validity—or, as Shakespeare (1597) writes in *Romeo and Juliet,* "That which we call a rose by any other name would smell as sweet" (2.2.43–44). Nonetheless, he adds that using different terminology for the same thing at times might be useful. The final researcher in the group suggests that researchers should reject validity and all other evaluation standards (Denzin, 2002). Discussions about reliability and generalizability would be no less problematic.

The following section in no way resolves the debate over the appropriate evaluative criteria for field research; rather, it presents an amalgam and not an exhaustive list of different perspectives.

Validity and Trustworthiness

Arguably, most field researchers concern themselves with what many of us refer to as *validity,* although they might not use this specific term. In place of *validity,* some researchers—particularly those who use an interpretive paradigm—substitute the concept of **trustworthiness** as the overarching evaluative standard for field research (Guba & Lincoln, 1994). Trustworthiness requires conducting and presenting the research in such a way that the reader can believe, or trust, the results and be convinced that the research is worthy of his or her attention (Lincoln & Guba, 1985).

Trustworthiness does not mean that the reader necessarily has to agree with the researcher; rather, it requires that the reader see how the researcher arrived at the conclusion he or she made. Without extensive field notes and other types of records to draw on, even the most experienced researcher will find trustworthiness difficult to establish. To achieve it, he or she must, at a minimum, communicate in detail the procedures used and the decisions made throughout the research process. Thus, the researcher interested in establishing trustworthiness should take care to include a detailed methods section in the final manuscript, as well as to connect the work to larger issues within the discipline.

The concept of trustworthiness possesses an embedded set of evaluative criteria, closely related and interdependent: **credibility, transferability, dependability,** and **confirmability.**

Internal Validity and Credibility

For some qualitative researchers, validity serves as the key evaluative criterion, particularly **internal validity,** a term that refers to the correspondence between what is reported and the social phenomena under study. The researcher achieves internal validity when he or she produces an accurate representation of the setting.

In general, field researchers argue that qualitative methodology has high internal validity; the in-depth and contextualized nature of qualitative research results in better and more nuanced understandings of the setting and its participants than is possible with quantitative research.

Beyond this global claim to internal validity, though, paradigmatic differences exist. For example, internal validity serves as an important criterion for judging qualitative research conducted under the post-positivist paradigm. The quest for high internal validity is consistent with the ontological perspective of this paradigm that there is some reality, or truth, that with appropriate methods can be captured. However, the issue of internal validity is somewhat problematic for researchers who adhere to paradigms other than post-positivism. If the ontological position of the researcher asserts that stable social reality does not exist, then the concept of internal validity cannot be applied in the same manner. As a way to avoid this ontological conundrum, many researchers have replaced internal validity with the criterion of credibility.

Credibility implies believability, authenticity, and plausibility of results (Miles & Huberman, 1994). For the reader to judge the results as credible, the methods used to collect and analyze the data must be seen as appropriate and rigorous, and the content of the final manuscript must be shown to have been derived from the data (Lincoln & Guba, 1985; Patton, 1999). A credible account rings true, both to the members in the setting and to the readers (Miles & Huberman, 1994). How does one achieve credibility? As mentioned previously, a detailed methods section helps establish it. Patton further suggests that the researcher's "training, experience, track record, status, and presentation of self" (p. 1190) enhance the credibility of the research. Other techniques for increasing the credibility of one's work, such as searching for negative cases and testing rival explanations, have been discussed elsewhere in this guide (Patton, 1999).

External Validity, Generalizability, and Transferability

Although field research can be generalizable, those who undertake it occasionally find **external validity**—the ability to **generalize** from a sample to a larger population or from one setting to another—difficult to achieve, even at times counterproductive to their efforts (Hoepfl, 1997). In fact, the very strength of field research—its focus on local conditions, specialized knowledge, in-depth accounts, and highly contextualized understanding of a setting—can decrease the degree of external validity. Consequently, in order to achieve high external validity, field researchers might have to sacrifice internal validity, a trade-off that many find themselves unwilling to make (Hoepfl, 1997; Lincoln & Guba, 1985).

The lack of comparable settings and small, nonprobability samples further erode the generalizability of some field research results. Field researchers accept this limitation. For example, Liebow (1994) writes, "[t]here is no claim that the women or the shelters here are representative of homeless women and shelters elsewhere" (p. 1).

Yet, field researchers generally hope that their work will have some implication beyond an understanding of the specific setting, as important as that might be. Liebow (1994) expresses this sentiment when he writes, "I do believe, however, that the problems the women face, and the dynamics of their relationship with one another and with others, do have relevance for other homeless women and for homeless men as well" (p. 1).

Knowing that external validity and generalizability often are problematic to some sorts of qualitative research, researchers occasionally reach for a substitute goal: transferability, a criteria that refers to the applicability of findings beyond the setting, situations, and participants included in the research (Stake, 1995). One type of transferability is known as **naturalistic generalizability** (Stake, 1995).

One of the key features distinguishing naturalistic generalizations from the more familiar statistical generalizations involves the fact that with the former, each individual reader determines whether the research findings are transferable, whereas the latter is a static characteristic of the research. Thus, the degree of transferability can vary depending on the experience, awareness, and knowledge of the reader. For example, take a single project read by two academics: an expert in the field and someone new to the discipline. The expert might find the research highly transferable, whereas the novice might find it low in transferability. Moreover, what one considers unimportant at one time might at a later date be considered highly transferable. The importance of the reader in the evaluative process does not mean, however, that the researcher cannot affect the degree of transferability of his or her research. On the contrary, the more details about a setting that the researcher provides, the more apt readers are to extrapolate the findings to other settings (Hoepfl, 1997).

A second type of transferability involves **analytic generalizations**, generalizing to a theory instead of to a larger population (Yin, 1993). Such generalizations occur when the researcher identifies concepts and social processes that have theoretical implications or significance beyond a specific setting. Locating one's research within an explicit conceptual and theoretical frame increases the likelihood of analytic generalizations.

Pershing's (2001) study of alleged honor code violations among women midshipmen at the Naval Academy provides an example of analytic generalizations. Pershing discovered three distinct factors that have implications for Kanter's (1977) theory of gender integration, which focuses on the entry of women into male-dominated civilian corporations. Pershing identified their high visibility, perceptions of them as sub-performers, and their lack of male friendship networks as contributing to the women midshipmen's overrepresentation as violators. The social process derived from Pershing's work both supports Kanter's theory and demonstrates the applicability of its insights to settings beyond the corporate world. Thus, Pershing made analytic generalizations from a specific setting to a well-known theory.

Reliability and Dependability

Another important criterion for evaluating research is reliability, which implies consistency. A bathroom scale is often used to explain reliability.

If your weight has not changed, a reliable scale will give the same result every time you step on it.

Reliable questions are those that, regardless of when they are asked, elicit the same responses from interviewees. Reliable respondents are those who provide consistent answers. Conclusions are reliable if different researchers draw similar ones from the same data. Although you can achieve reliability in a field setting, you might often find it unobtainable, not expected, and not necessarily a desired goal.

Because the lack of reliability is not always a problem for the qualitative researcher as it is for those who practice other methodologies, some researchers use the criterion of dependability as an alternative construct. If one's research is dependable, then the reader should have a context for understanding the lack of traditional reliability. Moreover, since dependability requires internal consistency among the core elements of the research project—research questions, data collection, analysis, and conceptual understanding—its presence helps ensure trustworthiness (Lincoln & Guba, 1985). To increase dependability, researchers create an audit trail, a detailed account of the entire research process that shows a correspondence between the methodology and the conclusions.

Objectivity, Value Neutrality, and Confirmability

Particularly among researchers who adhere to a post-positivist paradigm, objectivity and value-neutrality are important evaluative criteria. As a result, researchers try to make sure that their values, opinions, prejudices, or beliefs do not influence their research. In fact, the researcher's presence in the work often is that of the disinterested scientist. Otherwise, some claim that the research is biased.

In contrast to this value-free research approach, researchers operating within other paradigms view values as an inevitable, permissible, even desirable, part of research. Recognizing the subjective nature of field research, they replace objectivity and value-neutrality with confirmability, which requires that findings be supported by data. When working under the standard of confirmability, the researcher does not have to engage in the pretense of objectivity. Rather, he or she clearly articulates and embraces the role that values play in the research process. This does not imply that such researchers argue for the legitimacy of biased work. On the contrary, by centering their values and engaging in concerted reflections about their place in data collection and interpretation, researchers claim that they are in a better position to prevent bias.

Whether a rose is a rose, potatoes and potahtoes differ, or a rose would smell as sweet regardless of what it is called, field researchers engage in systematic procedures to help ensure the quality of their work.

Strategies for Enhancing Validity and Trustworthiness

As noted earlier, a good social scientist worries about the quality of a research project long before he or she enters the field. A number of distinct strategies, such as prolonged engagement in the field, reflexivity, thick descriptions, and triangulation (discussed previously), as well as member checking and peer and expert reviews (discussed in this section), help the researcher meet multiple standards. For example, a procedure that enhances credibility simultaneously helps establish internal validity, transferability, and confirmability. Although researchers use these techniques throughout the research process, member checking and peer and expert reviews become particularly important as the project nears completion.

Member Checking

For an analysis to be considered successful, it must ring true with two specific segments of the researcher's audience: members of the setting and colleagues who are experts on the topic (Fetterman, 1989, p. 21). There is a difference, however, between a description or finding that rings false, which probably means something is seriously amiss, and a controversial interpretation of the setting (pp. 21–22). The researcher who asks members of the setting to review a draft of the final manuscript will have an easier time distinguishing between the merely controversial and the downright wrong.

Stacey (1991) used member checking in her study of two families. Two members objected to what she had written. She notes,

> In the interval since we had spoken last, Pam and Dotty both had been reading drafts of the chapters I had written about their respective families. Neither was entirely pleased with what she had read. Dotty wished that I had not portrayed her family's plight in such disheartening terms. It was a depressing story, she agreed, but she would have given it a "more Pollyannaish" cast. However, Dotty observed, "It's your book, not mine." Pam had a comparable response. She had not yet finished reading all of the chapters, in part because she was finding doing so such an uncomfortable experience. Pam had detected a number of

minor factual errors in my portrait of her family. . . . Like Dotty, however, Pam had concluded that my textual errors were not her business. "After all," she reminded me, the book "is really not my baby; it's yours." (pp. xiii–xiv)

In this short paragraph, Stacey conveys several important points. First, Pam and Dotty did not totally agree with what she had written; such disagreement is not necessarily a problem, nor is it particularly uncommon. Second, neither Dotty nor Pam claimed ownership of the final project, which suggests that perhaps they felt less like collaborators in the project than objects of it, individuals to be written "about" or "for." Whether this represents a concern would depend on the researcher's paradigm. Third, we learn that Stacey stayed in contact with these women after she left the field. Fourth, because Stacey shared these comments with her readers, her work gains a measure of credibility. Finally, the report made Pam uncomfortable, a fact that reminds us in no uncertain terms that the way we write and share our work involves serious ethical issues.

What should you do if you discover that one or more of your participants disagree with the manner in which you have presented certain episodes or dispute the veracity of the facts? Prior to a member check it is important to clearly state if and how the member's input will be treated. Ultimately, researchers are not obligated to respond to requested changes, unless they have told the participants otherwise. Often, however, researchers feel compelled to take some sort of action if a reader responds negatively.

Sometimes researchers will include members' reactions as footnotes in the final versions of their manuscripts. In his study of homeless women, for example, Liebow (1994) asked two homeless women and the director of a shelter to write comments on his manuscript. He edited their comments for length but changed none of their language. In italicized footnotes on the relevant pages, he included some of the comments that confirmed his viewpoints and all the comments that disagreed with what he had written, that disagreed with each other, or that offered a different perspective (p. xvii). One such footnote, proffered by Grace, responds to a passage that states, "Many staff persons also offered consolation, encouragement, advice when asked, and a sympathetic ear" (p. 160). The footnote attributed to Grace reads,

Elliot lives in a dream world. He thinks all those staff people and volunteers were around to give love and help. I found some folks sincere in their efforts to help, others it seemed were there to be congratulated for being a volunteer. . . . The way people in authority treated you sometimes, I thought they were just out to rob me of what little I had left of my self-esteem. (p. 160)

In a similar manner, Bourgois (1995) used member checks, in part because of ethical concerns. He writes,

I also wanted to avoid excessively invading the privacy of the major characters in the book, and I discussed these issues at length with all of them. Only one person actually asked me to delete some material from the epilogue, which, of course, I did. The problems of selection, editing, and censorship have tremendous political, ethical, and personal ramifications that ethnographers must continually confront, without ever being confident of resolving them. (p. 342)

Regardless of the fact that many established researchers have encouraged members of a setting to read and comment on their final products, this procedure is not always possible or advisable (Stake, 1995). In some situations, once a study is completed, the members might not be accessible; in others, continued interaction is highly problematic. For example, in my evaluation of the Virtual Residential Program©, which provides services to seriously mentally ill youth and their families, contact with the clients after the completion of the program would have been inappropriate. Interviewing participants about the program after they were discharged might have prompted some of them to ask my advice regarding current problems they were experiencing, and my refusal to help could have been misinterpreted. I could not even refer them to the professionals from the Virtual Residential Program©, because they no longer had the required authorization to be in contact with the families.

Seeking feedback is often easier said than done. Duneier (1999) encountered some resistance when he attempted to read relevant parts of his book to the vendors. When he approached Keith, one of the vendors, he was unable to complete even a single sentence before Keith attempted to terminate the conversation. Further efforts only made Keith increasingly uninterested:

Keith: Man, do me a favor. Open the beer. . . . (p. 349)

Keith: . . . Give me the damn paper and damn pen and let me sign. . . .

Mitch: First, you gotta hear what the books says.

Keith: Oh, my God. Open the beer, please. This is getting on my nerves.

Mitch: First we gotta finish our work.

Keith: Damn that! I'm not signing nothing without no beer. (p. 350)

When Keith becomes inebriated, Duneier terminates the session, and only after contacting him three more times is Duneier able to read to him all relevant sections of the manuscript. Why was it so important for Duneier to seek Keith's input, particularly when he was so resistant? Duneier made multiple attempts to get Keith's response because he believes that he shouldn't publish something about someone that he "cannot look him or her in the eye and read" (1999, p. 351).

As you undertake your career in field research, remember that asking the participants you have interviewed, interacted with, and observed to review your work remains one of the many methods by which you can increase its validity and trustworthiness. You can further increase the quality of your research by relying on peer and expert reviews.

Peer Debriefing and Expert Reviews

Although most researchers find fieldwork a solitary pursuit, this does not negate the importance of seeking help from others, particularly a trusted peer or an expert in the topic. Frequent discussions with a colleague, committee member, or friend are part of the process known as **peer debriefing**, and in the research process they should begin early and occur frequently. **Expert reviews**, which involve seeking input from someone familiar with the research topic, perhaps even someone who has published on the subject, often occurs in the later stages of research.

Peer and expert reviewers use the paper trail, or dependability audit, as one of the mechanisms for checking consistency between a study's methodology and its conclusions. Detailed record-keeping and note-taking are vital to the process. One of the many reasons this guide has stressed the importance of documenting every aspect of the research is because of its utility in these reviews (Creswell, 1998).

Writing the Final Manuscript

Writing plays an essential role in all phases of field research (Denzin & Lincoln, 1994, p. 479). One does complete all the other stages of field research and then "write up" the results. Richardson (1994) reminds us,

Although we usually think about writing as a mode of "telling" about the social world, writing is not just a mopping-up activity at the end of a research project. Writing is also a way of "knowing"—a method of discovery and analysis.

I write because I want to find something out, I write in order to learn something that I didn't know before I wrote it. I was taught, however, as perhaps you were, too, not to write until I knew what I wanted to say, until my points were organized and outlined. (pp. 516–517)

Similar to Richardson, I view writing as yet another analytic strategy used by field researchers to gain insight into a setting. However, one major difference exists between the writing done throughout the field research process and that produced for the final manuscript: The latter must be well written by professional standards.

Novelist and critic Henry James is supposed to have said that there are only two kinds of books—those that are well written and those that are badly written. Although I'm inclined to think there are gray areas between the two extremes, I agree with the sentiment. In field research, writing serves as an analytic strategy, but this fact does not relieve the researcher from the need to conform to grammar rules, produce thesis statements and topic sentences, create well-organized paragraphs, or follow any of the other conventions of good writing.

But *truly* good writing goes far beyond conformity to rules and adherence to technical standards. Good writing requires writing and rewriting (and rewriting some more). It is not always fun, but it is almost always hard work! In fact, I agree with Michael Kanin, who said, "I don't like to write, but I love to have written" (ThinkExist.com, 2005).

Ueland provides good advice for moving you forward with your writing:

Writing, the creative effort, should come first—at least for some part of every day of your life. It is a wonderful blessing if you will use it. You will become happier, more enlightened, alive, impassioned, light-hearted, and generous to everybody else. Even your health will improve. Colds will disappear and all the other ailments of discouragement and boredom. (1938, as cited in Richardson, 2000, p. 940)

Although Ueland exaggerates the benefits of daily writing, writing every day is an excellent strategy. Your mind will become more flexible, your style more fluid, your vocabulary more mature. Eventually, even though you continue to struggle occasionally for a transition or search in vain for the perfect word, your confidence will improve. There is no guarantee you won't still get the flu, but at least your facility for language will improve.

Format of the Final Manuscript

Although you should strive to make your writing accessible to your intended readers, academic writing usually follows a style or pattern consistent with its disciplinary standards and methodology. As is the case with so many other aspects of field research, though, no single standard convention exists for the final manuscript. Instead, your presentation style will vary depending, in part, on your chosen paradigm. The format of the final manuscript evolves from essential ontological, epistemological, methodological and axiological assumptions. Numerous presentation formats exist with varying degrees of overlap. In this section, I summarize three writing styles, two at the opposite ends of the continuum of choices.

At one end of the spectrum one finds classical or traditional forms of ethnographic writing, sometimes referred to as **realist tales** (Van Maanen, 1988). Researchers who adopt this style write as if they perfectly capture the members' point of view and are able to give an accurate account of the setting. The researchers studiously omit details about themselves (Van Maanen, 1988). Van Maanen asserts that these manuscripts are "washed by a thick spray of objectivity" (1995, p. 7).

At the other end of the spectrum lie **experimental writings**. Although mainstream qualitative journals publish such writings, they are the most controversial of the styles presented here. For example, one type—the *narrative of the self*—reads not at all like a traditional ethnography because it uses the writing conventions of fiction. These free the researcher so he or she can "exaggerate, swagger, entertain, make a point without tedious documentation, relive the experiences, and say what might be unsayable in other circumstances" (Richardson, 1994, p. 521).

Note that forms of experimental writing that rely on fiction are *not* the same thing as the technique of analyzing one's data through crafting stories, as was presented in the last chapter. Field research stories are based in the data; the stories use the same conventions of fictions—dialogue, scenes, and so on—but what is told is not fiction. In contrast, experimental writing allows researchers to use their imaginations, to make things up if need be, to convey their points.

In between these two extremes is a style of writing that tends to be more tentative in its conclusions and more reflective in presentation than earlier forms of realist tales (Van Maanen, 1995). It also is more closely grounded in the data and the methodology of social science than experimental writings. The reader can gain a sense of the researcher and his or her place in the research, yet one does not get the sense that the focus of the research is the researcher. Those who use this style have moved from writing about "the other" to letting participants speak for themselves to focusing on the interdependence of the researcher and participants in the research process. The final manuscript is usually in the form of books and articles—not plays or poems. I classify most of the works cited in this guide as consistent with this style. Arguably, this genre is currently the dominant style for writing field research manuscripts.

As a researcher facing production of your final product, you will have to decide which form works best for you. The style you select will help determine how you will locate yourself, as the researcher, in the final manuscript.

Reflexivity and Objectivity

When writing the final manuscript, researchers decide to what degree their own voices will be heard. Field researchers working within the positivist tradition value objectivity and value neutrality. Therefore, their manuscripts are more apt to be written in the voice of the neutral observer, with few reflexive statements included in the final manuscript.

In contrast, the interpretive and critical paradigms possess an explicit epistemological assumption regarding the role of the researcher: What is learned about a setting and its participants is not independent of the researcher. Because of this epistemological assumption, the researcher is present in the text of the final manuscript.

"I" statements occur frequently. Researchers include reflections not just about the results of their analysis, but also about how they affected the research process itself and sometimes how the process affected them.

There is a difference, however, between locating oneself in the production of knowledge and being completely self-centered. Punch warns against opening "the floodgates for sentimental, emotional, pseudo-honest accounts detailing every nervous tremor and moment of depression or elation" (1986, p. 14). Another useful reminder is Bourgois's comment (perhaps more of a warning) that "[s]cholarly self-reflection often degenerates into narcissistic celebrations of privilege" (1995, p. 14).

Another important concern when writing the final manuscript is deciding to what degree the participants' voices are included.

The Participants' Voices

Simply put, I think the best final manuscripts are those that include generous helpings of the original dialogue of participants. Summarized and paraphrased accounts of conversations save time and space, but the original words of the participants help them come alive for readers. Take, for example, a telling selection from P. G. Wodehouse (1976). From this excerpt, one can see quite easily how two people can express essentially the same thought while saying something radically different about themselves. The first speaker is Bertram Wooster, a young man of privilege, and the second speaker is his butler, Jeeves:

Bertram: I've seldom had a sharper attack of euphoria. I feel full to the brim of Vitamin B. Mind you, don't know how long it will last. It's often when one's feelin' good that the storm clouds begin doing their stuff.

Jeeves: Very true, sir. Full many a glorious morning have I seen flatter the mountain tops with sovereign eye, kissing with golden face the meadows green, gilding pale streams with heavenly alchemy, Anon permit the basest clouds to ride with ugly rack on his celestial face and from the forlorn world his visage hide, stealing unseen to west with this disgrace.

Bertram: Exactly. I couldn't have said it better myself. You've got to watch out for a change in the weather. Still, you've got to be happy while you can.

Jeeves: Precisely, sir. Carpe diem, the Roman poet Horace advised. The English poet Herrick expressed the same sentiment when he suggested that we should gather rosebuds while we may. Your elbow is in the butter, sir. (Wodehouse, 1976, p. 404)

If I had been present as a field researcher observing this conversation, I could have summarized it in the final manuscript by saying that Jeeves and Bertram talked about how one needs to be prepared for quick and unexpected changes. Although this summary is technically correct, it does not capture the essence of this exchange with regard to language and style. Could you guess from my summary that Bertram, who speaks with much more casual diction and clumsily elbows the butter, is actually the young man of privilege, while Jeeves, whose speech is embellished with metaphor and classical allusions, is the butler? To understand these two men, one must hear them speak directly. The same holds true for representations in field research manuscripts.

Be forewarned, however: You will not find retaining the speakers' dialogue an easy task. You will often find yourself troubled by the syntactically twisted and grammatically skewed manner in which real people often speak. We talk in incomplete sentences, we halt in mid-sentence to reframe the same idea in different words, we trail off and leave thoughts uncompleted, we "hmmm" and "ahem" and "uh" our way through conversations. Our speech is filled with too many "you knows" and "I means." As a researcher, you will have the difficult task, at times, of wanting to include exactly what was said and how it was said and wanting to edit it for clarity. When you do edit dialogue, though, you should explicitly explain this action in your methods section or in a footnote. As if capturing the essence of an individual's speech is not enough to worry you, you will also find yourself walking the fine line between retaining the speaker's voice and ethical concerns.

Ethics

As you produce your final manuscript, inevitably you will face many ethical quandaries, about many of which this guide already has offered advice. Using names and locations in the final manuscript clearly violates confidentiality agreements if such agreements have been made. A more common breach of confidentiality involves using pseudonyms or references insufficient to disguise the source or place. For example, a reader might easily determine the location of a research setting once the institutional affiliation of the researcher is known, because researchers tend to choose sites close to home. This has led to the identification of Muncie, Indiana, as "Middletown," Seattle as "Rainfall West," and Oakland, California, as "Westville" (Punch, 1994). Further, what reads like an interesting but harmless detail or reference, such as the paint scheme on a motorcycle or the microbiological expertise of a respondent, may be sufficient for individuals thousands of miles from the research setting to identify a participant in the research. Liebow (1994) was rightfully concerned about confidentiality when he realized that Elsie, one of the homeless women he studied, could be identified easily from her physical description—"only one external ear, no ear canals, and a weight of over 300 pounds" (p. xviii). Rather than risk violating confidentiality, he sought and received permission to identify her. If he had not received Elsie's permission, he would not have included descriptions of her.

Researchers must consider the long- and short-term implications of what they write. Bourgois (1995), for example, was so worried that his portrayal of the poor might reinforce negative stereotypes that he carefully explained his rationale for including in his book what he referred to as "the dark side of poverty" (p. 11). Although researchers should not feel compelled to sugar-coat reality or paint a positive image of participants in the setting, they should consider the ethical implications of their renditions.

As has probably become clear to you by now, completing a field research project from inception to final manuscript is a challenging yet exciting task. Should you get this far, it is a major accomplishment worth celebrating.

Conclusion

At this point, we have traveled together a long way on our journey into field research. Although your work as a researcher might be just beginning, you should now have a better sense of how to gain an understanding of everyday life in a setting through long-term interactions with the people you meet there. I hope this guide both has given you an appreciation for the complexity and utility of field research and will serve as a handrail to steady your steps as you progress into the exciting but difficult terrain of your own research project.

I want to reassure you that in spite of the difficulties and ambiguities of this type of research, you are more than capable of undertaking such a project, even at this early stage of your career. Field research is not an activity that should be restricted to an elite few. It involves careful preparation, adherence to ethical standards, intense interaction, thorough data collection, rigorous analysis, and polished writing—tasks that any of us can complete capably given time and determination. I strongly encourage you to engage in field research because that is the best way to learn how to conduct field research.

Chapter Highlights

1. Field researchers strive to engage in research that is valid and/or trustworthy.

2. Not all researchers agree on what criteria should be used to evaluate field research.

3. Some researchers prioritize validity, generalizability, and reliability as standards for evaluation.

4. Trustworthiness, credibility, transferability, dependability, and confirmability are used as evaluative standards by some researchers.

5. Field researchers frequently share their final report with participants to see if it rings true to them.

6. Peer debriefing and expert reviews can help ensure the validity and trustworthiness of field research.

7. Including the participants' dialogue in the final manuscript increases the validity and trustworthiness of one's research.

8. Researchers need to decide to what degree they will include themselves in their final manuscript.

9. Ethical issues are salient throughout the field research process, including the final manuscript.

Exercises

1. Field researchers debate about which set of evaluative standards is appropriate for judging field research. Indicate whether you think validity, reliability, and generalizability or trustworthiness, credibility, dependability, transferability, and confirmability are more appropriate. Justify your answer.

2. Explore journals that primarily publish qualitative research. Find two articles that use radically different writing styles. Describe the two styles. Which do you like best and why?

3. Some qualitative researchers include reflexive accounts and clearly locate themselves in the final manuscript. Others are less inclined to so do. Write a paragraph using "I" statements that argues for the place of the researcher in the final manuscript. Write a second paragraph, arguing that the researcher should be the "invisible" author. In this paragraph, do not refer to yourself. Then indicate which of these two views you find most compelling. Which style did you find easier to write?

References

Abrams, J. (Producer). (2004). *Lost* [Television series]. Burbank, CA: ABC.

Altheide, D., & Johnson, J. (1994). Criteria for assessing interpretive validity in qualitative research. In N. Denzin & Y. Lincoln (Eds.), *Handbook of qualitative research* (pp. 485–499). Thousand Oaks, CA: Sage.

American Anthropological Association. (n.d.). *AAA ethics*. Retrieved July 18, 2005, from http://www.aaanet.org/committees/ethics/ethics.htm

American Sociological Association. (1999). *Code of ethics and policies and procedures of the ASA committee on professional ethics*. Washington, DC: Author.

Arnado, M. (2002). *Class inequality among third world women wage earners: Mistresses and maids in the Philippines*. Unpublished doctoral dissertation, Virginia Tech, Blacksburg.

Atkinson, P., & Hammersley, M. (1994). Ethnography and participant observations. In N. Denzin & Y. Lincoln (Eds.), *Handbook of qualitative research* (pp. 248–261). Thousand Oaks, CA: Sage.

Bourgois, P. (1995). *In search of respect: Selling crack in El Barrio*. Cambridge, UK: Cambridge University Press.

Bulmer, M. (1982). *Social research ethics*. London: Macmillan.

Bulwer-Lytton, E. (1830/2004). *Paul Clifford*. Rockville, MD: Wildside.

Burgess, R. G. (1991). Sponsors, gatekeepers, members, and friends: Access in educational settings. In W. Shaffir & R. Stebbins (Eds.), *Experiencing fieldwork: An inside view of qualitative research* (pp. 43–52). New York: St. Martin's Press.

Burroway, J. (2003). *Writing fiction: A guide to narrative craft* (6th ed.). New York: Longman.

Chapman, R. (2003). Endangering safe motherhood in Mozambique: Prenatal care as pregnancy risk. *Social Science and Medicine, 57*, 355–375.

Chenault, T. (2004). *"We did it for the kids," housing policies, race, and class: An ethnographic case study of a resident council in a public housing neighborhood*. Unpublished doctoral dissertation, Virginia Tech, Blacksburg.

Creswell, J. (1998). *Qualitative inquiry and research design: Choosing among five traditions*. Thousand Oaks, CA: Sage.

Denzin, N. (2002). Confronting ethnography's crisis of representation. *Journal of Contemporary Ethnography, 31*, 482–490.

Denzin, N., & Lincoln, Y. (1994). Part V: The art of interpretation, evaluation, and presentation. In N. Denzin & Y. Lincoln (Eds.), *Handbook of qualitative research* (pp. 479–483). Thousand Oaks, CA: Sage.

Denzin, N., & Lincoln, Y. (2003). Part II: Paradigms and perspectives in transition. In N. Denzin & Y. Lincoln (Eds.), *The landscape of qualitative research: Theories and issues* (2nd ed., pp. 245–252). Thousand Oaks, CA: Sage.

DiFranco, A. (1993). Willing to fight. On *Puddle dive* [CD]. Buffalo, NY: Righteous Babe.

DiFranco, A. (1995). Crime for crime. On *Not a pretty girl* [CD]. Buffalo, NY: Righteous Babe.

DiFranco, A. (1999). Trickle down. On *Up, up, up, up, up, up* [CD]. Buffalo, NY: Righteous Babe.

DiFranco, A. (2004). True story of what was. On *Educated guess* [CD]. Buffalo, NY: Righteous Babe.

DiFranco, A. (2005). Paradigm. On *Knuckle down* [CD]. Buffalo, NY: Righteous Babe.

Duneier, M. (1999). *Sidewalk*. New York: Farrar, Straus and Giroux.

Ellis, R. (2002). *A feminist qualitative study of female self-mutilation*. Unpublished master's thesis, Virginia Tech, Blacksburg.

Emerson, R. (1988). *Contemporary field research: A collection of readings*. Prospect Heights, IL: Waveland.

Esterberg, K. (2002). *Qualitative methods in social research*. Boston: McGraw-Hill.

Ferron, S. (1980). Ain't life a brook. *Testimony* [Cassette recording]. Oakland, CA: Redwood Records.

Fetterman, D. (1982). Ethnography in educational research: The dynamics of diffusion. *Educational Researcher, 11,*17–29.

Fetterman, D. (1989). *Ethnography: Step by step*. Newbury Park, CA: Sage.

Flick, U. (1999). *An introduction to qualitative research*. London: Sage.

Flick, U. (2002). *An introduction to qualitative research* (2nd ed.). London: Sage.

Flick, U., von Kardorff, E., & Steinke, I. (2004). What is qualitative research? An introduction to the field. In U. Flick, E. von Kardorff, & I. Steinke (Eds.), *A companion to qualitative research* (pp. 3–11). London: Sage.

Fontana, A., & Frey, J. (1994). Interviewing: The art of science. In N. Denzin & Y. Lincoln (Eds.), *Handbook of qualitative research* (pp. 361–376). Thousand Oaks, CA: Sage.

Galliher, J. F. (1982). The protection of human subjects: A re-examination of the professional code of ethics. In M. Bulmer (Ed.), *Social research ethics* (pp. 152–165). London: Macmillan.

Gans, H. J. (1962). *The urban villagers: Group and class in the life of Italian-Americans*. New York: Free Press.

Garrahy, D., Kulinna, P., & Cothran, D. (2005). Voices from the trenches: An exploration of teachers' management knowledge. *The Journal of Education Research, 99,* 56–63.

Geertz, C. (1973). *The interpretation of cultures*. New York: Basic Books.

General Accounting Office. (1990). *Case study evaluations*. Retrieved January 9, 2005, from http://www.gao.gov/special.pubs/pe1019.pdf

Gershwin, G. (music), & Gershwin, I. (lyrics). (1937). Let's call the whole thing off. Performed by F. Astaire and G. Rogers in *Shall we dance* [Motion picture]. RKO Pictures.

Gold, R. (1969). Roles in sociological field observation. In G. McCall & J. Simmons (Eds.), *Issues in participant observation* (pp. 30–38). Reading, MA: Addison-Wesley.

Golde, P. (1986). Odyssey of encounter. In P. Golde (Ed.), *Women in the field: Anthropological experiences* (pp. 67–93). Berkeley: University of California Press.

Gongaware, T. (2003). Collective memories and collective identities: Maintaining unity in Native American educational social movements. *Journal of Contemporary Ethnography, 32,* 483–521.

Grimm, J., & Grimm, W. (1955). *Grimm's fairy tales.* New York: Random House.

Guba, E., & Lincoln, Y. (1994). Competing paradigms in qualitative research. In N. Denzin & Y. Lincoln (Eds.), *Handbook of qualitative research* (pp. 105–117). Thousand Oaks, CA: Sage.

Hamm, J. (2003). *We can't die without letting them know we were there: Oral histories of Konnarock Training School alumnae and faculty.* Unpublished doctoral dissertation, Virginia Tech, Blacksburg.

Hammersley, M. (1992). *What's wrong with ethnography?: Methodological explorations.* London: Routledge.

Hesse-Biber, S., & Leavy, P. (2006). *The practice of qualitative research.* Thousand Oaks, CA: Sage.

Hoepfl, M. (1997). Choosing qualitative research: A primer for technology education researchers. *Journal of Technology Education, 9,* 47–63.

Hopper, C., & Moore, J. (1994). Women in outlaw motorcycle gangs. In P. Adler & P. Adler (Eds.), *Constructions of deviance: Social power, context, and interaction* (pp. 389–401). Belmont, CA: Wadsworth.

Humphreys, L. (1970). *Tearoom trade: Impersonal sex in public places.* New York: Aldine de Gruter.

Johnson, J. (1975). *Doing field research.* London: Free Press.

Jorgensen, D. (1989). *Participant observation: A methodology for human studies.* Newbury Park, CA: Sage.

Junker, B. (1960). *Field work.* Chicago: University of Chicago Press.

Kanter, R. (1977). *Men and women of the corporation.* New York: Basic Books.

Kershaw, T. (2005). *The scholar activist approach.* Retrieved December 15, 2005, from http://www.africanastudies.vt.edu/The%20Scholar%20Activist%20Approach.htm

Klinenberg, E. (2002). *Heat wave: A social autopsy of disaster in Chicago.* Chicago: University of Chicago Press.

Krieger, S. (1985). Beyond "subjectivity": The uses of the self in social science. *Qualitative Sociology, 8,* 309–324.

Kvale, S. (1996). *InterViews: An introduction to qualitative research interviews.* Thousand Oaks, CA: Sage.

Lawson, H. (2000). *Ladies of the lot*. Boston: Rowman & Littlefield.

Levi, M. (2003). Faith and practice: Bringing religion, music and Beethoven to life in Soka Gakkai. *Social Science Japan Journal, 6*, 161–180.

Lewins, A., & Silver, C. (2005). *Choosing a CAQDAS package: A working paper*. Retrieved January 5, 2006, from http://caqdas.soc.surrey.ac.uk/ChoosingLewins&SilverV3Nov05.pdf

Lewis, N. (2005). *A study of intra-racial violence among black males: A matter of 'diss'respect*. Unpublished doctoral dissertation, Virginia Tech, Blacksburg.

Liebow, E. (1994). *Tell them who I am: The lives of homeless women*. New York: The Free Press.

Lincoln, Y., & Guba, E. (1985). *Naturalistic inquiry*. Beverly Hills, CA: Sage.

Lincoln, Y., & Guba, E. (2003). Paradigmatic controversies, contradictions, and emerging confluences. In N. Denzin & Y. Lincoln (Eds.), *The landscape of qualitative research: Theories and issues* (2nd ed., pp. 283–291). Thousand Oaks, CA: Sage.

Lofland, J. (1971). *Analyzing social settings*. Belmont, CA: Wadsworth.

Lofland, J., & Lofland, L. (1984). *Analyzing social settings: A guide to qualitative observation and analysis* (2nd ed.). Belmont, CA: Wadsworth.

Lofland, J., & Lofland, L. (1995). *Analyzing social settings: A guide to qualitative observation and analysis* (3rd ed.). Belmont, CA: Wadsworth.

Macabuac, M. (2005). *After the aquaculture bust: Impacts of the globalized food chain on poor Philippine fishing households*. Unpublished doctoral dissertation, Virginia Tech, Blacksburg.

Martineau, H. (1838/1989). *How to observe morals and manners*. New Brunswick, NJ: Transaction.

McGuire, S. (1998). *At-risk, first-year students' patterns of perceptions of their academic performance activities and grades earned*. Unpublished doctoral dissertation, Virginia Tech, Blacksburg.

Melville, H. (1851). *Moby-Dick; or, the whale*. London: Harper and Brothers.

Miles, M., & Huberman, A. M. (1994). *Qualitative data analysis: An expanded sourcebook* (2nd ed.). Thousand Oaks, CA: Sage.

Miller, E. (1986). *Street woman*. Philadelphia: Temple University Press.

Morse, J., & Richards, L. (2002). *Readme first for a user's guide to qualitative methods*. Thousand Oaks, CA: Sage.

Myers, J. (1994). Non-mainstream body modification: Genital piercing, branding, burning, and cutting. In P. Adler and P. Adler (Eds.), *Constructions of deviance: Social power, context, and interaction* (pp. 414–446). Belmont, CA: Wadsworth.

Neuman, W. L. (1991). *Social research methods: Qualitative and quantitative approaches*. Boston: Allyn & Bacon.

Newman, K. (1999). *No shame in my game: The working poor in the inner city*. New York: Knopf.

Nichols, J. (1974). *The Milagro beanfield war*. New York: Ballantine Books.

Norris, L. (2000). Interior country. In *Toy guns* (pp. 9–20). Kansas City: Helicon Nine Editions.

Oakley, A. (1981). Interviewing women: A contradiction in terms. In H. Roberts (Ed.), *Doing feminist research* (pp. 30–61). London: Routledge & Kegan Paul.

Ortiz, S. (2004). Leaving the private world of wives of professional athletes: A male sociologist's reflections. *Journal of Contemporary Ethnography, 33,* 466–488.

Parkhill, T. (1993). What's taking place: Neighborhood *Ramlilas* in Banaras. In B. Hertel & C. Humes (Eds.), *Living Banaras: Hindu religion in culture context* (pp. 103–126). Albany: State University of New York Press.

Patton, M. (1990). *Qualitative evaluation and research methods* (2nd ed.). Newbury Park, CA: Sage.

Patton, M. (1997). *Utilization-focused evaluation: The new century text* (3rd ed.). Thousand Oaks, CA: Sage.

Patton, M. (1999). Enhancing the quality and credibility of qualitative analysis. *Health Services Research, 34,* 1189–1208.

Pershing, J. (2001). Gender disparities in enforcing the honor concept at the US Naval Academy. *Armed Forces and Society: An Interdisciplinary Journal, 27,* 419–449.

Phan, T. (2005). Interdependent self: Self-perceptions of Vietnamese-American youths. *Adolescence, 40,* 425–441.

Porter, E. (1913). *Pollyanna.* Boston: L C. Page & Company.

Prus, R., & Irini, S. (1988). *Hookers, rounders, and desk clerks: The social organization of the hotel community.* Salem, WI: Sheffield.

Punch, M. (1986). *The politics and ethics of fieldwork.* Beverly Hills, CA: Sage.

Punch, M. (1994). Politics and ethics in qualitative research. In N. Denzin & Y. Lincoln (Eds.), *Handbook of qualitative research* (pp. 83–98). Thousand Oaks, CA: Sage.

Richardson, L. (1994). Writing: A method of inquiry. In N. Denzin & Y. Lincoln (Eds.), *Handbook of qualitative research* (pp. 516–529). Thousand Oaks, CA: Sage.

Richardson, L. (2000). Writing: A method of inquiry. In N. Denzin & Y. Lincoln (Eds.), *Handbook of qualitative research* (2nd ed., pp. 923–948). Thousand Oaks, CA: Sage.

Roadburg, A. (1980). Breaking relationships with research subjects: Some problems and suggestions. In W. Shaffir, R. Stebbins, & A. Turowetz (Eds.), *Fieldwork experience: Qualitative approaches to social research* (pp. 281–291). New York: St. Martin's Press.

Rosecrance, J. (1990). You can't tell the players without a scorecard: A typology of horse players. In C. Bryant (Ed.), *Deviant behavior: Readings in the sociology of norm violations* (pp. 348–370). New York: Hemisphere.

Roy, A. (1997). *The god of small things.* New York: Random House.

Russell, B. (1991). *Silent sisters: A study of homeless women.* New York: Hemisphere.

Ryan, G., & Bernard, H. (2003). Data management and analysis method. In N. Denzin & Y. Lincoln (Eds.), *Collecting and interpreting qualitative material* (pp. 259–309). Thousand Oaks, CA: Sage.

Scarce, R. (1994). (No) trial (but) tribulations: When courts and ethnography conflict. *Journal of Contemporary Ethnography, 23,* 123–149.

Schwandt, T. (2001). *Dictionary of qualitative inquiry* (2nd ed.). Thousand Oaks, CA: Sage.

Shakespeare, W. (1597/1969). *Romeo and Juliet.* In A. Harbage (Ed.), *William Shakespeare: The complete works* (pp. 858–893). Baltimore: Penguin Books.

Sieber, J. (1982). *The ethics of social research: Fieldwork, regulation, and publication.* New York: Springer.

Solis, J. (2003). Re-thinking illegality as a violence *against,* not *by* Mexican immigrants, children, and youth. *Journal of Social Issues, 59,* 15–31.

Spradley, J. (1980). *Participant observation.* Belmont, CA: Wadsworth.

Stacey, J. (1991). *Brave new families: Stories of domestic upheaval in late twentieth century America.* New York: Basic Books.

Stake, R. (1995). *The art of case study research.* Thousand Oaks, CA: Sage.

Stake, R. (2004). *Standards-based & responsive evaluation.* Thousand Oaks, CA: Sage.

Stein, A. (2001). *The stranger next door: The story of a small community's battle over sex, faith, and civil rights.* Boston: Beacon Press.

Stein, G. (1922). Sacred Emily. In *Geography and plays* (pp. 178–188). Boston: Four Seas.

Strauss, A. (1987). *Qualitative analysis for social scientists.* Cambridge, UK: Cambridge University Press.

Strauss, A., & Corbin, J. (1990). *Basics of qualitative research: Grounded theory procedures and techniques.* Newbury Park, CA: Sage.

Sundberg, J. (2004). Identities in the making: Conservation, gender and race in the Maya Biosphere Reserve, Guatemala. *Gender, Place and Culture—A Journal of Feminist Geography, 11,* 43–67.

Tarasuk, V., & Eakin, J. (2003). Charitable food assistance as symbolic gesture: An ethnographic study of food banks in Ontario. *Social Science and Medicine, 56,* 1505–1515.

Taylor, S., & Bogdan, R. (1998). *Introduction to qualitative research methods* (2nd ed.). New York: John Wiley & Sons.

ThinkExist.com Quotations. (2005). Retrieved August 12, 2005, from http://en .thinkexist.com

Thompson, H. S. (1979). *Gonzo papers: Vol. 1. The great shark hunt.* New York: Fawcett Popular Library.

Trauger, A. (2004). Because they can do the work: Women farmers in sustainable agriculture in Pennsylvania, USA. *Gender, Place and Culture—A Journal of Feminist Geography, 11,* 289–308.

Ueland, B. (1938). *If you want to write: A book about art, independence and spirit.* St. Paul, MN: Graywolf.

van den Berghe, P. (1968). Research in South Africa. In G. Sjoberg (Ed.), *Ethics, politics and social research* (pp. 183–197). Cambridge, MA: Schenkman.

Van Maanen, J. (1982). Fieldwork on the beat: This being an account of the manners and customs of an ethnographer in an American police department. In J. Van Maanen, J. Dabbs, Jr., & R. Faulkner (Eds.), *Varieties of qualitative research* (pp. 103–151). Beverly Hills, CA: Sage.

Van Maanen, J. (1988). *Tales of the field: On writing ethnography.* Chicago: University of Chicago Press.

Van Maanen, J. (1995). An end to innocence: The ethnography of ethnography. In J. Van Maanen (Ed.), *Representation in ethnography* (pp. 1–35). Thousand Oaks, CA: Sage.

Wacquant, L. (2002). Scrutinizing the street: Poverty, morality, and the pitfalls of urban ethnography. *The American Journal of Sociology, 107,* 1468–1534.

Warren, C. (1988). *Gender issues in field research.* Newbury Park, CA: Sage.

Warren, C., & Karner, T. (2005). *Discovering qualitative methods: Field research, interviews, and analysis.* Los Angeles: Roxbury.

Wax, R. (1971). *Doing fieldwork: Warnings and advice.* Chicago: University of Chicago Press.

Weitzman, E. (1999). Analyzing qualitative data with computer software. *Health Services Research, 34,* 1231–1263.

Welty, E. (1994). Place in fiction. In *Collected essays.* New York. Retrieved February 1, 2006, from http://xroads.virginia.edu/~drbr/welty.txt

Whyte, W. F. (1955). *Street corner society: The social structure of an Italian slum* (2nd ed.). Chicago: University of Chicago Press.

Wilson, G. (2005). This doesn't look familiar! A supervisor's guide for observing co-teachers. *Intervention in School and Clinic, 40,* 271–275.

Wodehouse, P. (1976). *Jeeves, Jeeves, Jeeves.* New York: Avon.

Wolburg, J. (2001). The 'risky business' of binge drinking among college students: Using risk models for PSAs and anti-drinking campaigns. *Journal of Advertising, 30,* 23–40.

Wolcott, H. (1990). Making a study "more ethnographic." *Journal of Contemporary Ethnography, 19,* 44–72.

Wolcott, H. (1994). *Transforming qualitative data: Description, analysis, and interpretation.* Thousand Oaks, CA: Sage.

Yin, R. (1994). *Case study research: Design and methods* (2nd ed.). Thousand Oaks, CA: Sage.

Glossary/Index